Joy of Scrapbooking

Joy of Scrapbooking

by Lisa Bearnson & Gayle Humpherys

Oxmoor House®

Creating Keepsakes™ Joy of Scrapbooking

Copyright © 1998 Porch Swing Publishing, Inc., and Blackberry Press, Inc.
Published by Oxmoor House, Inc., and Leisure Arts, Inc.
Oxmoor House, Inc., Book Division of Southern Progress Corporation,
P.O. Box 2463, Birmingham, Alabama 35201

A Blackberry Press Book

Library of Congress Catalogue Card number: 98-66930
Hardcover ISBN: 0-8487-1829-1
Softcover ISBN: 0-8487-1840-2
Manufactured in the United States of America
First Printing 1998

Creating Keepsakes™ is a registered trademark of Porch Swing Publishing, Inc., P.O. Box 2119, Orem, Utah 84059-2119, (888) 247-5282.

We're Here for You!
We at Oxmoor House are dedicated to serving you with reliable information that expands your imagination and enriches your life. We welcome your comments and suggestions. Please write us at:

Oxmoor House, Inc.
Editor, Creating Keepsakes™ Joy of Scrapbooking
2100 Lakeshore Drive
Birmingham, AL 35209

To order additional publications, call 1-205-877-6560.

Oxmoor House, Inc.
Editor-in-Chief: Nancy Fitzpatrick Wyatt
Senior Crafts Editor: Susan Ramey Cleveland
Senior Editor, Editorial Services: Olivia Kindig Wells
Art Director: James Boone

Blackberry Press, Inc.
Washington, D.C.
President: Maureen Graney
Creative Director: Carmile S. Zaino
Illustrations: Jackie Pardo
Designer: Kevin Callahan/BNGO Books
Editors: Moira Duggan, Laura Morris, Sonia Reece Myrick
Production Consultant: Patricia J. Upchurch
Index: Pat Woodruff

Cover photograph of Lisa Bearnson by Grant Heaton Photography, Salt Lake City, Utah, and art directed by Don Lambson.

Background paper pattern, pages 132 to 156: Courtesy of The Paper Patch, Riverton, Utah. (Available colors will vary.)

Joy
of
Scrapbooking

Contents

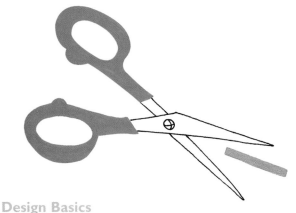

An Idea Book for Inspiration, 131

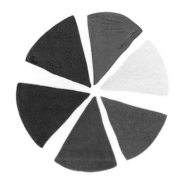

Why I Love Making Scrapbooks

LAST FALL MY FAMILY took a lazy Sunday drive in the mountains near my home. We chatted happily about life, and my children ooed and aahed over the spectacular colors of the leaves. A moment of silence was suddenly interrupted by my three-year-old, Collin, who said: Isn't it great to be with the whole family? I immediately got teary-eyed and was touched by this profound statement from someone so small.

Moments and experiences like these are priceless but if they aren't recorded they'll mesh into other memories and eventually be forgotten. The layout shown on this page will help my family remember that day for generations to come. The leaves (preserved with acid-free laminate), accompanied by photographs and mixed with my family's recollections, make for a pretty great page. Even better, the layout provides a memory that will last through the ages.

As the editor of *Creating Keepsakes*, a national magazine devoted to the art of preserving memories, I know that scrapbooking can be as meaningful to you and your family as it is to ours. I've had the opportunity to pore over thousands of scrapbook pages sent in by readers everywhere and share their wonderful enthusiasm for the hobby.

In celebration of this spirit, writer Gayle Humpherys and I have gathered together into one encyclopedic volume the best scrapbook page ideas and tips from *Creating Keepsakes* since its inception. Then, we added sixty all-new scrapbook designs that have never appeared in print in a special section at the end. We want new and experienced scrapbookers alike to be as up-to-date as possible on all the best ideas available today. Scrapbooking will bring loads of fun into your life today—and its rewards for you and your loved ones will last more than a lifetime.

HELPS FAMILY MEMBERS FEEL IMPORTANT

Several times a week, my children look through their scrapbooks and say, "I

Photo: Patrick Kerry Studio, Provo, Utah. Scissors: Family Treasures (Deckle); Leaf punch: McGill; Corner decorative punch: McGill.

Laminate (to preserve leaves): Therm O Web.

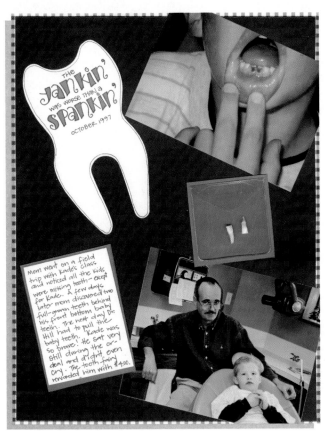

Gingham paper: The Paper Patch; Die Cut: Ellison; Memorabilia Pocket: 3L.

Cookie paper: Geo; Sticker: Stickopotamus; Punches (cookies and chocolate chips): McGill.

remember when this happened" or "I remember when we did this!" In my opinion, nothing promotes self-esteem more than a child or even a grownup looking through his or her own scrapbook. Everyone loves to feel important, and what better way than to have someone be the star of his or her own book?

A few months ago, my seven-year-old, Kade, had two teeth pulled. Of course I captured the moment on film. I then commemorated his bravery by putting the story, photos and teeth on a scrapbook page. (I saved the teeth in an acid-free memorabilia pocket.) Kade shows this page (above) to anyone who comes through our front door! He loves to show off the picture of his war wounds and point out the wording that says he didn't even cry when the dentist was pulling the teeth!

CONNECTS THE GENERATIONS

Every time Collin goes to my mom's house, he begs to make cookies with her. More often than not, Grandma gets out her mixing bowl and they spend the next hour making tasty treats. Luckily my mom has taken snapshots of some of these cookie-making episodes. When she last gave me photos, I wanted to create the perfect page so Collin would know how much he was loved by his grandma. After a little brainstorming, I knew what would make the page complete—a personalized note from Grandma. And, what better background to have her write it on than a "From the Kitchen of Grandma" recipe card?

This scrapbook page (above, right) is one of my favorites. Although simple in design, it focuses on the most

important part of scrapbooking—the photos and the story behind the photos. It also contains a priceless heirloom—a personal note to Collin in my mom's own handwriting—that will be cherished for years to come.

PROVIDES A PERFECT OUTLET FOR CREATIVITY

Scrapbooking is the perfect way for me to unleash my creativity. Best of all, the pages already have a place in my home (in a binder in sheet protectors), they never need to be dusted (yippee!), and they never go out of style. Most importantly I'm using my time on something worthwhile that will last more than a lifetime.

Now, what are you waiting for? Dig out those photos, turn on your imagination, and let's begin!

—LISA BEARNSON

JAMIE, KELAN AND KYLIE

WE'RE BUMPIN' UP AND DOWN IN OUR...

JAMISON

Creating Your Keepsake

Preserve precious photos and memories for generations to come

The summer I was seven, my mom presented me with a huge red photo album and said, "Why don't you put a scrapbook together?" She'd carefully saved my school pictures and artwork, so putting together the scrapbook was easy and fun. But the materials I used—clear tape, construction paper, rubber cement, and felt-tip and ball-point pens—are now causing that precious heirloom to crumble literally before my eyes.

Thank goodness those days are gone forever. Now there's a plethora of photo-safe, archival, and acid-free supplies on the market. The following pages contain "must have" information for every type of scrapbooker—novice, intermediate, and experienced. You'll love the tips on getting started and innovative advice on saving money, organizing your materials, and storing memorabilia. Best of all, you'll learn how to be confident that the scrapbooks you create today will remain completely intact for generations to come.

By Barbara Silvester. Paper and wagon cut-out: Paper Pizazz, Hot Off The Press; Fonts: "Medfly" from 2000 Fantastic Fonts, Expert Software "TypeTwister," Aldus; Computer Clip Art: Microsoft Publisher. (See Index for complete spread.)

What You Need to Get Started

• • • • • • • • • • Essential Supplies • • • • • • • • • •

JUST WHAT EXACTLY *do* you need to start creating a scrapbook? If you look through a scrapbook store or catalog, you'll find literally hundreds of different supplies available—a selection that can be a little overwhelming to a beginner. But before you start buying things right and left, take a minute to learn which tools are most important. You might find that you already own several of them, such as scissors, adhesives, and a permanent-ink pen. And, while many of the supplies you see in stores and catalogs make working with scrapbooks easier and more enjoyable, there are really only a handful of essential items that you need to get started. Once you've got those, you can continue to add other fun items to your supply barrel a few at a time. So, let's take a brief look at six of the most basic supplies.

PAPER

Paper is one of the necessary items for creating a scrapbook, and it comes in a huge variety of colors, designs, weights, and textures. Paper not only provides the backbone for each page, it can also be cut and folded in hundreds of different ways to add color and dimension throughout your album. Heavier paper, such as cardstock, is best used as the base for an entire page as well as the backing for photographs or other papers. Lightweight paper, such as patterned paper, is easily folded, cut, or torn into designs to frame the photos and embellish the page.

For starters, find a variety pack of cardstock in the colors you like (such as brights or country colors). These packs usually come in 50 or 100 sheets and will give you a good starting supply. In addition, if your album doesn't already have pages in it, you'll need at least 25 sheets of white cardstock. Then, you can add to your paper supply with additional colors and patterns as you need them.

When choosing paper for your scrapbook, it's important to pay attention to the paper's acidity level. Different papers contain varying degrees of acid that can destroy photographs over time. However, many papers now available are virtually acid-free and safe for use in a scrapbook. If you're not sure whether a specific paper type is photosafe, you can test it with a pH testing pen (see page 33). For more information on the different paper types available, see the "Paper" section on page 66.

SCISSORS

Another basic tool for constructing a scrapbook is a good pair of straight scissors. Scissors are used to trim photos, cut photo frames from cardstock or other paper, and create other paper designs and shapes. For making quick, straight cuts, you can use an X-Acto knife or paper trimmer in place of scissors. If you make a lot of small, precise cuts, you might find a pair of scissors with a fine tip to be helpful (such as those used for embroidery). There are also many other fun cutting tools available, such as scissors with decorative edges, circle cutters, and rotary cutters. To learn more about these and other options, see the "Scissors" section on page 70.

you only need a few items to get started

Interesting paper, coordinating die cuts, and decorative-edge scissors are supplies that make scrapbooking fun. By Cindy Bess, Chandler, Arizona. Paper: The Paper Patch, D.O.T.S.; Pens: Sakura Micron Pigma; Scissors: Fiskars (Peaks); Die Cuts: Ellison.

ADHESIVES

Of course, you need to have some way to attach your photos and other designs to each page, and that's where adhesives come in. As with the other scrapbook supplies, there are a lot of different options when it comes to deciding which type of adhesive to use. Glues and other kinds of adhesives vary not only in the way they are applied (such as a liquid glue pen vs. photo corners) but also in their photo-safe qualities and how long they last. Make sure you select an adhesive that is nontoxic and acid-free, such as a glue stick, double-sided tape, or photo corners. See the "Adhesives" section on page 72 for more information about the different choices available for securing items in your album.

One of the easiest adhesives for beginners to use is the "photo split"— a small double-sided sticker; they usually come in boxes of 500. Photo splits are quick to apply and hold your photos securely, although they can be removed if necessary.

PENS

Once you've arranged your photos on a scrapbook page, it's important that you add a title to the page and labels describing the event taking place (a process called *journaling*). Doing so will add tremendous value to the photos and memories. All it takes is a permanent pen! And with so many different styles and colors of pens, markers, and colored pencils to choose from, it's easy to add decorative and attractive lettering to your pages.

For starters, you should have a basic fine-tip pen with permanent black ink. This pen can be used to write labels for the photos and events on the page. Of course, you can add variety to your pages by using other pens in different styles and colors, as well as by using different lettering techniques. Another helpful tool is a blue photo-marking pencil, which you can use to label the backs of photos. Always make sure that the pens you use in your albums are permanent, photo-safe, waterproof, fade-resistant, and quick-drying. Nonpermanent pens can smear if moisture comes into contact with the page, leading to devastating results. For more information about lettering tools and techniques, see the section beginning on page 102.

BINDERS

A binder or album allows you to store and organize all of your scrapbook pages in one location. Binders come in many different styles and sizes, and choosing the best one for you is largely a matter of personal preference. Two of the most popular choices for scrapbookers are three-ring binders and expandable-spine albums. In a three-ring binder, individual pages are kept in page protectors and can easily be inserted, taken out, and rearranged. You can also choose a different background color for each page. Expandable-spine albums already contain good archival-quality pages of a single background color (generally white) and are often a slightly larger size. Pages can also be added or removed from these albums.

When choosing a binder, first decide what size you want your pages to be. Generally, three-ring binders use 8.5″ x 11″ pages, while expandable-spine albums use larger pages, such as 12″ x 12″, although you can find both album types in other sizes. Another choice is the spiral-bound album. This type is available in different sizes and provides more permanent storage for your scrapbook pages. (Individual

By Debbie O'Connor, New Baltimore, Michigan. Paper: Creative Memories; Scissors: Fiskars (Victorian); Stickers: Mrs. Grossman's; Die Cuts: Ellison; Ruler: Borderlines Wavy, Creative Memories.

book, you can begin to acquire some of the other products that make this hobby so much fun. You don't have to go out and buy all these products at once—instead, add one at a time and share supplies with friends. Below is a brief description of some of the products that can help enliven your scrapbook pages. You'll find more specific information about these products in the "Tools and Techniques" section, beginning on page 66.

Decorative Scissors • These are special scissors in dozens of different edge designs—from zigzags to ripples to scallops. Use decorative scissors to quickly create unique edges around your photos, photo frames, lettering, and other shapes. The possibilities are endless!

Stickers • You can find virtually acid-free stickers today for practically any occasion. They come in almost any style, shape, size, or color and are simple to apply. You'll use stickers to enhance the overall theme of your page, as well as to fill in empty spaces.

Punches • Paper punches are a quick way to add motifs and small designs to your album pages. Punches come in a wide variety of shapes, such as hearts, stars, bears, trains, and more. Punches also vary in size, and you can even purchase punches specially designed for adding designs to the corners of a page or photo. In addition, punches give you a great way to make use of your paper scraps.

Templates • Your photos can easily be cut into different shapes with the help of

pages are not easily added, though.) To learn more about the different types of binders and albums, see the section beginning on page 36.

SHEET PROTECTORS

A final necessity for creating a scrapbook is sheet protectors. These protectors keep dust, oily fingers, food spills, and other outside elements from harming your photographs. If you're using a three-ring binder, the punched page protectors also allow you to store your pages in the binder. Expandable-spine albums also have page protectors avail-

able that fit the album. (Currently, spiral-bound albums do not provide page protectors.) Sheet protectors are readily available at office supply stores, as well as craft and scrapbook stores. Start with a box of 50, and make sure that the sheet protectors you choose are archivally safe—most plastics *other* than PVC (polyvinyl chloride) are photo-safe, such as polyethylene or polypropylene. (See page 26 for more information.)

OTHER FUN SUPPLIES

After you've assembled the basic supplies to get started making a scrap-

templates. Common template shapes include circles, ovals, and hearts. You can also find templates for unusual shapes, such as flowers and Christmas trees. Most templates consist of a thin plastic sheet with several sizes of a similar shape cut out from it. This allows you to trace the best shape around a photo and crop out unwanted backgrounds.

Die Cuts • Similar to stickers and punches, die cuts can add color to a page, fill up empty space, and help to carry a page's theme. Die cuts are available in a wide assortment of shapes and sizes and can be cut from any type of paper. You can purchase precut shapes or, if available, use a die-cut machine at a local scrapbook store to cut out your own.

Clip Art • Clip art is a collection of related images created by a professional artist. Clip-art styles range from classic to cute—there are images to fit almost any occasion. If you have a computer, you can print out the images you want from a clip-art software package. You can also purchase "cut and copy" books and copy the images on a photocopier. After printing or copying the images, you can add color if you want to complement the photos on the page.

Rubber Stamps • Rubber stamping is a hobby in itself, but stamping can also greatly enhance your scrapbook pages by adding color and dimension. Stamping techniques such as embossing and masking have many different applications in a scrapbook. When using stamps, make sure the ink is permanent and acid-free (whether it's from an ink pad or from markers). To learn more about stamping, see page 112.

Now that your supply bin is filled with all the right scrapbooking tools, you're ready to get to work. In the coming pages, you'll learn how to put everything together and preserve all your wonderful memories!

On a Budget?

IT'S NO SECRET that purchasing scrapbook supplies can get expensive. But just because you can't afford to run out and buy every neat tool you see, that doesn't mean you can't still create a great scrapbook. If you're working on a budget, here are some tips to save you a few dollars along the way:

- Work on your scrapbook with friends or family so you can share and pool your supplies. That way, not everyone needs to buy her own sailboat punch or paper trimmer.

- Swap extra supplies or things you no longer use with other scrapbookers.

- Look for sales and coupons. If you get a discount for buying large quantities, have a friend or two split the order with you. Also, shop around at office supply, discount, and fabric stores for lower prices on some of the more common items such as paper, scissors, and stickers.

- Save all of your paper scraps and use them for punching out designs, backing smaller photos, and cutting out shapes.

- If you are using cardstock as a border around a page or photo, save the part you cut out for other uses.

- Make your own templates by tracing cookie cutters onto poster board and then cutting the designs out with an X-Acto knife.

- If you use double-sided photo splits as an adhesive, cut them into pieces for mounting smaller photos or die cuts.

- Save greeting cards and wrapping paper to use for cutting out designs and punches (make sure you test them first for acidity levels with a pH testing pen).

- If you have a computer and access to the Internet, you can find free computer fonts and clip art, layout ideas, and lots of other scrapbook-related information.

- When purchasing pens or markers, buy only one at first. After trying it out and making sure you like the feel and results, go back and buy additional colors.

- Trace your own clip art from a child's coloring book. (Hold the paper up to a lighted window for better tracing visibility.)

- When processing your film, have duplicates made, especially if you have separate albums for your children. Duplicates are much cheaper than reprints made later.

• • • • •Tips for the Beginning Scrapbooker• • • •

AS YOU START on your scrapbook-making journey, just looking at the growing piles of photos in boxes and drawers can be enough to make you ask yourself, "What was I *thinking?*" It's common for new scrapbookers to feel a little frustration and discouragement from time to time, especially as they try to get organized and find time for their albums. If you've felt similar obstacles, take a deep breath and then follow the tips below to help you get started, get organized, and get the most out of your scrapbooks.

DECIDE WHAT ALBUMS YOU WANT TO CREATE

An important first step in putting together your scrapbooks is to decide what types of albums you want to end up with. Do you want just a family album? Separate albums for holidays and vacations? Individual books for each family member? Deciding which types of albums you want to create beforehand greatly speeds up the process of sorting and organizing your photographs. If you need some ideas for the different types of albums you can create, see the sections beginning on page 36.

SORT AND STORE YOUR PHOTOS

Probably the most time-consuming task is organizing all of your photographs and other memorabilia. However, once this step is done, you'll find that your scrapbook work will move much quicker. First, gather all of your photos and then sort them according to the albums you're putting together. Then, sort the photos further according to date or subject. If it hasn't already been done, label the backs of each photo with the date and the names of the people pictured, using a blue photo-marking pencil.

After you've sorted all the photos, find a safe storage location until you're ready to put them in your scrapbook. You can use photo-safe boxes, file folders, or large envelopes. Keep the sorted categories and dates together and make sure that the container doesn't have a high acid content so it won't harm your photos. For more information on different ways to organize and store your photographs and memorabilia, see the sections beginning on pages 18 and 22.

WORK BACKWARD

Although it may seem like a strange concept at first, one of the best ways to create a scrapbook is to work backward. In other words, start with your most recent photos and then gradually work back through your older photos. Not only will you be able to remember more details about the newer photos while the memories are still fresh, but you'll have a greater sense of accomplishment.

DO ONE PAGE AT A TIME

Don't try to do your whole album in one sitting. Instead, focus on completing one page at a time. A great way to work on a page at a time is to place all the photos, stickers, paper, and other items that you want to use for a particular page in a sheet protector. Then,

Die-cut images and frames, patterned papers, decorative-edge scissors, and photos are basic supplies that can be used in hundreds of creative ways. By Brenda Hall, Mesa, Arizona.

do one page at a time

when you have a few minutes, all you need to do is grab the page protector and you have everything you need to get right to work.

In addition, decide how much time you can afford to spend on each page. If you find yourself spending several hours to get a single page just right, you might want to focus more on recording the memories rather than getting too caught up in the page decorations.

LEAVE YOUR SUPPLIES SET UP

If you can, find a spot to set up your scrapbooking materials—whether it's a corner in your bedroom, the living room, or the kitchen—and then keep them out, ready for use. Then, whenever you have a few minutes of spare time, you can sit down and work without having to drag out your supplies and put them away again when you're finished (a process that can take as much time as you spend actually working on your albums). If you have small children, you might need to store your materials in a room that can be locked.

If you can't leave your supplies permanently set up, store the bulk of your supplies in a central location (such as a closet) and keep the smaller supplies that you use more often in a small tote or case that can easily be carried. When you're ready to work, just grab your small supply case (refill it with any supplies, if needed) and you're all set!

INVOLVE YOUR FAMILY AND FRIENDS

One way to really speed up the process of completing your albums is to enlist the help of your family and friends. Get your older children (including the married ones), other family members or relatives, or close friends to help you sort photos and put together the album pages. Don't worry if the pages aren't done exactly the way you'd do them—the important thing is that the memories are being recorded. An added bonus is that each page will be a unique reflection of its creator. Kids of practically any age can also start their very own albums (duplicate photos are great for this). You'll be surprised how creative they are!

MAKE TIME FOR SCRAPBOOKING

Finally, remember that just as in other hobbies, you need to make the time to work on your scrapbooks. If you don't make your scrapbooks a priority, you'll constantly find other projects to fill up your days. Some people find they need to actually schedule the time on their calendars or planners. Try to choose a consistent time each week or month to work on your albums. Many scrapbookers get together with a group of friends on a monthly basis (or more often) to share supplies and ideas. Find the time that works best in your schedule and stick with it!

A Word to the Wise

JUST AS THERE ARE a lot of helpful tips for getting your albums started, there are also a few things you *shouldn't* do. Avoid these common mistakes:

- Don't store your photos in the older "magnetic" albums with sticky pages and thin plastic coverings. These albums contain high degrees of acid that can ruin your photos. If you have photos in magnetic albums, remove them and store them in envelopes until you're ready to put them in your new albums.

- Don't crop or silhouette every picture. Full-size pictures can add a lot to a page and you also might be cutting out fun background details.

- Don't use ballpoint pens to label the backs of your photos. This can cause indentations or smearing on other photos. Instead, use a blue photo-marking pencil for labeling.

- Don't feel like you have to use every picture in your album. Choose the best photos for your album and store the remaining photos in an acid-free box, or give them to friends or family.

- Don't let the stickers, die cuts, and other decorations on a page overshadow the pictures and journaling. The pictures and the written memories should be the main focus.

Collecting and Organizing

• • • • • • • • • • • • • Photographs • • • • • • • • • • • • • •

ONE OF THE BEST things you can do to make the entire scrapbooking process run smoother is to start by organizing your photographs. This important step is often the most time-consuming (and at times, the most overwhelming), but once it's been tackled, you'll enjoy focusing on the fun aspects of recording your memories on scrapbook pages. Plus, you'll feel a tremendous sense of accomplishment just making it to that point! There are lots of different ways you can organize your photos, as well as lots of choices for storing the photos once they've been sorted.

MAKE THE TIME

Since the task of organizing your photos can be quite time-consuming, you need to make it a priority. Otherwise, you're bound to find countless other projects sneaking in to fill up your schedule. Don't hesitate to take several afternoons or an entire Saturday to start digging into those piles of photos. Pencil it in on your calendar if necessary to make sure you stick with your scheduled time. After all, the work you're doing is important in preserving your family's history.

At the same time, remember that scrapbooking is not a race. Even if you can only fit in an afternoon or two each month for working on photos, keep with it until the organizing process is complete. Work at your own pace—don't get discouraged—and the job will be done before you know it.

acid-free boxes are great for storing photos

SORT, SORT, SORT!

Before you start sorting, find a large work area where you can spread things out and, preferably, leave them out. The kitchen table probably isn't the best location because you'll find yourself spending lots of time cleaning things up (and then getting them back out again next time). By leaving your "sorting piles" out, you'll be able to concentrate all of your available time on the task at hand and to easily work in a few extra minutes here and there.

Next, gather all of your photos together at your work area. You might also want to track down negatives, memorabilia, and other keepsakes, which can be sorted at the same time. Look through all of your favorite storage spots (such as drawers and closets)

to make sure you haven't forgotten anything. If your photos are already stored in albums, all you need to do is collect the albums and then remove the photos as you sort them into the various piles. (For photos that are stuck in the older "magnetic" albums, try using dental floss to remove them without damage.)

Now you're ready to sort. There are several different ways you can group your photos as you sort them. The best method for you depends largely on the type of albums you want to create. For example, if you're creating a Christmas-theme album, you should sort all of your Christmas pictures together. Similarly, if you're creating a separate album for each family member, you'll want to create sorting piles for each person. Here are some ideas for ways to sort your photos:

Chronologically • For this method, start by sorting the photos into piles according to year, then break down each year into months or events (such as Christmas or vacations) within that year.

By Family Member • Sort the photos into separate piles for each family member, based on who is featured in the picture (or whose album you want the photo placed in). You might also have piles for general family pictures and miscellaneous pictures that aren't specific to a family member. Double (or even triple) prints are very helpful

for this type of sorting, since many pictures can go into more than one person's pile. If you want to include a picture in multiple piles and don't have extra copies of it, set it aside in a reprint pile.

By Subject • Make piles of your photos according to subjects or events, such as holidays, vacations, birthdays, outdoor activities (sports, trips to the park, etc.), and school activities.

You can combine any of these sorting methods, if you like. For example, after sorting according to family member, you might sort each person's pile chronologically. If you have a large number of photos, start

by sorting into very general piles, such as decades (1980's) or life experiences (college, marriage before kids, etc.); then, sort each large group into smaller piles, such as individual years or events.

LABEL THE PHOTOS

After you've finished sorting, go through the piles and label any photos that haven't already been identified. Labeling the backs of photos is an important step for two reasons. First, it might be a while before you create the actual scrapbook page for a particular photo, and it's easy to forget the specific details. And second, if your photos ever become separated from

By Gwendy Kem, Scottsdale, Arizona. Scissors: Fiskars (Pinking) and Family Treasures (Jumbo Deckle); Stickers: Creative Memories.

By Janae Goerz, Menomonee Falls, Wisconsin. Pens: Sakura Micron Pigma; Stickers: Mrs. Grossman's, Creative Memories, Sandylion.

the scrapbook page, you'll be able to identify them easily.

Here are a few helpful guidelines for labeling your photos:

• Use a blue photo-marking pencil or an acid-free permanent-ink pen. There are also specific photographic markers available. Don't use ballpoints on photos: they can cause indentations and possibly bleeding of ink through the photo.

• Include the date the photo was taken and the names of the people pictured. If possible, record the place and a *brief* description of the event.

• If you're using a marker or pen, make sure no other photo comes in contact with the ink before it is dry. The ink on the back of one photo could trans-fer to the front of another picture.

• If you have a computer, you can print the photo information on adhesive labels (make sure they're acid-free), and then just stick the labels on the backs of the photos. This is a quick way to label duplicate photos.

STORAGE OPTIONS

Now that you've got your photos sorted and labeled, you need to store them safely until you're ready to put them in your scrapbook. You also need permanent storage for any photos that you *don't* end up using in an album. There are lots of different options for storing your photos safely.

Photo Boxes • Sturdy boxes designed to hold and organize your snapshots are available in different sizes, but generally hold 500 to 1,000 photos (4″ x 6″ or smaller). In addition, they often come with divider tabs and labels for keeping your photo-filing system organized. Smaller boxes can be stacked on top of each other, and larger units with individual drawers are also available. Acid-free boxes are a great way to store photos that you don't plan to use in your albums.

File Folders • File folders (either hanging files or manila folders) are an easy way to keep sorted photos related to a specific event, time period, or person in the same place. For example, you can place your Christmas photos in separate manila file folders for each year, and then place all the folders in a single hanging file labeled "Christmas." Or, if you've sorted your photos chronologically, use folders for each month, holiday, or event within each year. Store the folders in a filing cabinet, file-folder box, or file tote. Choose a container with a lid to keep out dust.

Accordion Folders • Expandable accordion folders can also be used to store your sorted piles of photos. Use one folder for each year, category, or family member, and, if you want, include individual manila file folders within each accordion folder.

Clasp Envelopes • Large envelopes with a clasp are another good option for storing your categorized photos. In addition to photos, you can easily include programs, ticket stubs, and so on, in the envelope. This helps you keep everything together in one place. (For more ideas on storing memorabilia items, see "Memorabilia" on page 22.)

Sheet Protectors • If you plan to create your album in a three-ring binder, consider storing your photos in individual sheet protectors. Simply place the photos you want to use on a single page in a sheet protector, along with any paper, stickers, die cuts, or other supplies. Store the sheet protectors in your binder, and when you're ready to create a page, all you need to do is pull one out. This method works great for scrapbooking "on the go," but make sure you store the binder upright!

Cases and Carts • A variety of different storage cases and carts are available on the market, including products created specifically for scrapbookers. For example, you'll find portable cases, carts on wheels, and stackable storage boxes. Often, these items are designed to hold photos as well as scrapbook supplies.

You may be able to find items that are already around your house—such as folders or small boxes—to store your organized photos, but you'll want to check that they are archivally safe. For long-term storage, wood containers should be avoided, as well as anything containing acid or PVC (polyvinyl chloride). For more information on materials and conditions that are harmful to photos, see "Basic Conservation Principles" on page 26.

Whichever storage method you choose for your photos, make sure that you label each sorted category clearly so you can quickly find the photos you need. Don't store the containers in an area of high humidity or where there are extreme temperature changes, such as an attic or basement. In addition, try to avoid direct sunlight, dust, and dirt. A good storage location is a closet that is not bounded by any exterior walls.

KEEP IT UPDATED

Whew! You've conquered those piles of photos and put everything away in its place. Now, keep your system updated by sorting, labeling, and storing new photos as soon as you get them developed. Having a good storage system in place will help you update your files quickly.

Organization is one of the keys to successful scrapbooking. By taking the time now to sort through your photos and establish a filing method that works for you, you'll be able to relax and take your time putting together your albums, feeling confident that you'll know where things are when you want them.

Storing Your Negatives

NEGATIVES ARE JUST as important as photos and there are many benefits to organizing them and storing them safely. Negatives allow you to replace lost or damaged prints, and are the best way to get reprints made (although a lab can create a copy of a photo using just the original print). Here are some tips for storing and organizing negatives:

- Acid-free envelopes can be used to store negatives. Often, negatives are returned from the developer in suitable envelopes. Make sure you label the outside of each envelope with the date or event.

- Negative sleeves let you store your negatives in full-sized pages that can be placed in a binder for easy organization. In addition, negative sleeves let you easily view your negatives without having to worry about fingerprints or scratches.

- Many film developers now offer photo files, which are proof sheets that show a reduced image of each picture from a roll of film. This is the fastest way to find pictures for reprints, since you don't have to hold the negatives up to light to find the correct reorder number.

- Store your negatives in a separate location from your photos. That way, if something ever happens to either your photos or negatives, you haven't lost everything. You might even consider storing your negatives in a fireproof safe or safe-deposit box, or at a relative's home.

• • • • • • • • • • • • Memorabilia • • • • • • • • • • • •

PHOTOGRAPHS AREN'T the only things that can be organized in a scrapbook. Memorabilia can greatly enhance your albums. Mementos such as programs, handwritten notes, pressed flowers, fabric swatches, embroidery, and coins can bring life to the photographs and recorded stories—and be safely stored at the same time. Even keepsake items that are too large for a scrapbook can be included through photographs and journaling.

The process of collecting, organizing, and storing memorabilia doesn't just apply to heirloom items passed down through generations—it's one you can continue today. Special keepsakes give a tangible, personal touch to the stories on your scrapbook pages. Here are some ideas for finding and organizing items that will add value, interest, and fun to your scrapbook.

WHAT TO COLLECT

Some people are naturally inclined to save souvenirs (although keeping track of them might be another story). Others don't see a need to hang on to certain items, or they simply don't think about it. If you fall in the first category and tend to be a pack rat, your focus might be more on deciding what *not* to keep from the items you've collected.

If collecting hasn't been easy for you in the past, start today to look consciously for things you can add to your scrapbook. Take a look at other people's albums, and use some of the ideas below to get started. Remember, you don't have to save *everything*—just those items that have the most importance to you. And the more scrapbook pages you create, the more you'll find yourself noticing items and thinking, "Hey! That would make a perfect addition to my scrapbook!"

Just because an item isn't initially flat doesn't mean you can't later include it in your scrapbook. (The section "Including Memorabilia in Scrapbooks" on page 32 will give you lots of ideas.) Keep your eyes open for mementos, such as the items below, that might make a meaningful addi-

it's great to be organized

tion to your album—and don't forget to take the pictures to accompany them!

Special Occasions and Events • Special occasions and holidays are a perfect time to gather memorabilia. Wedding and graduation announcements, party invitations, and favors are some common mementos. Boutonnieres and corsages can be kept if dried carefully. Save a piece of your favorite costume or the name cards from your Thanksgiving dinner. And don't overlook ticket stubs, programs, and playbills from a night on the town.

New Family Members • A new baby is always a welcome sight and a great reason to create scrapbook pages! Hang on to your ultrasound photos, hospital masks and bracelets, and newborn stocking caps. Baby booties or socks can adorn a scrapbook page, along with hair ribbons or a penny from the year of the birth. Consider including a corner from a favorite security blanket (when the blanket's all worn out), a swatch of fabric from the baby's blessing dress, or a lock of hair from that first haircut.

Vacations • When you're traveling, pick up some maps, travel brochures, and pamphlets about the areas and attractions you visit.

By Barbara Tanner, Sandy, Utah. The background paper is a color copy of a watercolor painting Sara Tanner made at her preschool.

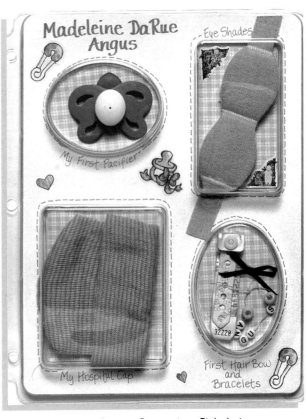

By Tiffani D. Angus, Darien, Connecticut. Pink designer paper: The Paper Patch; Stickers: Melissa Neufeld (corners); Provo Craft (baby items). Keepsake Keeper: Design Vinyl.

Grab business cards from your favorite shops or restaurants. (This also helps you remember the exact business name.) Postcards are a great way to show things you missed with your camera. Don't forget hotel stationery, ticket stubs, and collectible buttons or pins. If you're vacationing abroad, save some of the foreign coins and currency or postage stamps.

Kid Stuff • Kids can quickly fill up a room with all the stuff they bring home. Save your children's *favorite* artwork, stories, and other school projects. (Let them pick one or two to keep in addition to the ones you choose.) Keep track of special valentines, cards, and handwritten notes. What about including the first missing teeth along with a picture of the toothless grin?

Items from Nature • When you're outdoors taking pictures, pick up a few leaves or flowers to add texture and life to your scrapbook pages. A trip to the beach can result in a treasure of seashells or even some plain old sand! Gather some pine cones or pebbles along the way. (Take extra care in storing and preserving flowers, leaves, and other organic material properly.)

Family Favorites • Save memorabilia that have special significance, such as a monogrammed handkerchief, charm bracelets, buttons, or pins. Everyday items can also help tell a story. For example, include a swatch of fabric from the new curtains you made, or a piece of linoleum from your kitchen remodeling project. Hold on to receipts of special items purchased. (You'll be amazed years later at how inexpensive they were!)

By Karla Vos, Bellflower, California. Paper trimmer: Fiskars (Deckle).

Records and Awards • Certificates, ribbons, and awards help showcase a person's unique talents. You can create eye-catching scrapbook pages using scout badges or high-school varsity letters. Other fun records to keep include old or expired ID cards, report cards, and pertinent newspaper or magazine articles. Finally, don't forget to add some personality to your pages with handwritten notes and letters.

ORGANIZING AND STORING MEMORABILIA

Now that you've started collecting all of this "stuff," what do you do with it? If you simply toss it into a box or drawer, it's likely to be either damaged or forgotten. And will you really be able to remember that those wildflowers came from your hike up the canyon on July 13? Organizing your memorabilia will help you keep track of everything so you can include it on the right scrapbook page. In addition, storing your mementos safely helps you preserve them as long as possible.

Depending on how you've organized your photos, you might find it easiest to store certain memorabilia items directly with any accompanying photos. That way, you won't forget about them when it's time to create that particular page. For example, you can use a large clasp envelope or an accordion-style envelope to keep associated mementos and photos together, such as all of the photos, ticket stubs, travel brochures, and other keepsake items from a summer vacation. Or, place them all in a sheet protector with the stickers, die cuts, and other items you want to use when you create your page. However, be careful about storing items that are sharp-edged or highly acidic (such as newspaper clippings) directly with photographs.

For mementos that you don't store directly with your photos, list their location and description on an index card, and place the card (or other note) with the associated photos. Then, keep the items in a sturdy container with a lid to keep dust out. For long-term storage of larger items, an acid-free, lignin-free box is the best option.

With any memorabilia item that you keep, record the date and other pertinent information, such as the name of the person who created or owned the item, the location where it was collected, and other details that tell the story behind it. Depending on the item, this can be recorded on the back of the object, on the envelope or box it's stored in, or on a piece of acid-free paper that's stored with the item. Don't attach things to fabric with safety pins or paper clips, as they might cause rust or other damage.

With your memorabilia organized, you'll know right where to find them when you're ready to create your scrapbook page. See "Including Memorabilia in Scrapbooks" on page 32 for ideas on how to safely incorporate your mementos into your album.

Including memorabilia in your scrapbook allows you to enjoy and relive—in a tangible way—memories that might otherwise have faded. These special keepsakes are sure to add the perfect touch to the photos in your scrapbook.

By Marilyn Anderson, Layton, Utah.

What to Save and What to Throw Out

As you sort through the stash of papers, memorabilia, and other keepsakes that you've managed to collect, it can be tough deciding which items are worth keeping. Here are a few helpful guidelines:

● Don't try to save everything from a special occasion or event. Select one or two items that have the most meaning to you and toss the rest.

● If you don't have any photos to accompany a memento, or if there isn't a unique story behind it, throw it out.

● Keep items that help tell the story behind the accompanying photographs or provide insights into what you *can't* see in the pictures.

● If an item has special sentimental value to you or a family member, hang on to it, no matter what others might say. As you periodically evaluate your collection over the years, decide if that item still has as much meaning to you. If not, you can get rid of it at that time.

● After photographing a large item that's too bulky to be included in your scrapbook, decide if it's something that you still want or need to keep.

● Heirlooms and other items that represent family traditions or legacies are worth keeping and even passing on to your children.

● Keep items that are unique or extraordinary. These items often have a story to tell in and of themselves!

● For artwork and other school projects created by children, keep those that the children are especially proud of, those that showcase different talents or abilities, and those that appeal to you. In addition, include at least one handwriting sample.

3 Preserving Photos and Documents

• • • • • • Basic Conservation Principles • • • • • •

PHOTOGRAPHS, journals, letters, and mementos help us keep even our most distant memories in mind. While some of these items naturally last longer than others, all of them are subject to some type of decay and deterioration, especially if they are not taken care of properly. By becoming familiar with some of the things that lead to deterioration, you can better keep and protect your keepsakes so they'll last for generations to come.

WHAT CAUSES DETERIORATION?

At a basic level, all items are made up of chemical bonds. If these bonds start to break down—either in reaction to another chemical substance or from chemical reactions within the material itself—an item will lose its present form and perhaps decompose. By being aware of elements and environments that weaken chemical bonds or speed up the deterioration process, you can more safely preserve and extend the life of an item. Here are a few things to watch out for:

Acid • Acid is a substance that can weaken the bonds of many materials,

such as paper and fabric, causing them to turn brown and become brittle over time. Acid is often left in a material incidentally from chemicals used during the manufacturing process. In addition, acid can migrate into a substance from other materials that come in contact with the item. (More about the different sources of acid is given a little later.)

Heat • High temperatures can speed up the chemical reactions within a material, causing it to decay more quickly. Photographs and film are especially affected by high temperatures.

Humidity • High humidity can adversely impact many materials, since the extra moisture in the environment encourages the growth of fungus and mold. Damage can also occur when there are large fluctuations in humidity levels—such as might occur in an attic, basement, or garage. These conditions cause the materials to continually expand and contract.

Light • Bright light—especially sunlight and fluorescent light—can harm many materials. Like heat, the light

speeds up chemical reactions and the deterioration process. In addition, light fades ink and bleaches colors. Photographs are particularly susceptible to bright light, since film is inherently a light-sensitive material.

Careless Handling • Another common cause of damage to documents and photographs is careless handling. Oils and dirt from our hands can transfer to the materials and mishandling or improper storage often leads to scratches, rips, and tears.

SOURCES OF ACID

Acid is known to cause harm to documents and photographs, and people are more aware than ever of the need for proper acid-free storage. Since acid can come from a variety of different sources, it's important to check all of the products you use in your scrapbook. For example, if you use acid-free paper in your scrapbook, but include an item with a high acid content, such as a newspaper clipping, other items in your scrapbook can become contaminated. Here are some common sources of acid:

Low-Quality Paper • Cheaper paper, such as newsprint, often contains high degrees of acid from its manufacturing process. Other types of paper that you might include in your scrapbook, such as ticket stubs or letters, might also be acidic.

Certain Adhesives • Some types of adhesives—especially older adhesives like rubber cement and cellophane tape—are highly acidic and can damage your photos and documents. In addition, the adhesive used in older "magnetic" albums (those with self-adhesive boards behind clear plastic sheets) is extremely harmful to photos. Over time, your documents and photos can actually be absorbed into the adhesive, making them extremely difficult to remove.

PVC • Polyvinyl chloride is used in certain plastic products, such as some types of sheet protectors. PVC and other harmful "plasticizers" can also

be found in some adhesives, as well as in the older "magnetic" albums. Over time, PVC breaks down to form hydrochloric acid.

Lignin • Lignin is an organic substance that occurs naturally in wood and plants. When wood is broken down to create paper, lignin fibers often remain in the paper (unless they are removed through a special manufacturing process). Over time, lignin can break down into acids, causing the paper to turn brown and brittle.

Lignin is especially common in cheaper paper such as newsprint.

STEPS TO PROPER PRESERVATION

What can you do to keep your scrapbook and photographs safe? Here are a few simple preservation steps—more specific suggestions for documents, photos, and memorabilia are also given in the next several sections.

- Store your scrapbook and photographs away from bright light, inconsistent temperatures, and high humidity.
- Use acid-free (or pH-neutral) materials in your scrapbook. In chemistry, a pH value of 7.0 is neutral—lower values are acidic and higher values are alkaline (acid-free). If you're unsure about a paper's acid content, you can test it with a pH testing pen.
- Make sure any adhesive you use is acid-free or pH-neutral.
- Avoid anything containing PVC (polyvinyl chloride). Instead, look for items that contain polyethylene, polypropylene, or polyester (such as Mylar, which is considered one of the best materials for archival plastic envelopes and sheet protectors).
- Use paper with a lignin content of less than 1%. These papers are generally labeled "lignin-free."
- If you have items that are slightly acidic or contain some lignin, you can slow the deterioration process down a little by using buffered paper. Buffered paper is pH-neutral paper that has had calcium carbonate

added to it to make it more alkaline. This helps neutralize any acids that might occur from the breakdown of lignin in the paper or that migrate to the paper from other sources. However, buffered paper is not meant to absorb large amounts of acid.

Protect your photographs and documents from deterioration. But remember to keep things in perspective and not get overly anxious about the materials used in your scrapbook. Become familiar with the best storage techniques and products available, and then simply enjoy the creative process of preserving your memories in a scrapbook!

• • • • • • • Old and New Photographs • • • • • •

FOR MORE THAN 150 years, photographs have helped us capture moments in time, creating memories that families cherish for generations. Because the methods of photography and processing have changed dramatically over those 150 years, many different types of photographs can be found today. Fortunately, it's possible for both old and new photographs to last for decades—even centuries—with the proper care. Becoming familiar with the best storage conditions for photographs will help you enjoy them for many years to come.

ANTIQUE PHOTOS

In the early days of photography, the continual discovery of new camera methods and processing techniques resulted in several different types of photographs. Certain types of photographs were more common because of their inexpensive cost and ease of processing. Some of these older photos include the following:

Daguerreotypes • Among the very first photographs, daguerreotypes

daguerreotype

were popular from 1839 to about 1860. These photographs use a thin, silver-coated metal sheet and have a highly polished, mirrorlike surface. They are sealed in glass and were often placed in small, hinged cases. Daguerreotypes should *never* be disassembled.

Card-Mounted Photos • During the latter part of the 19th century, card-mounted photographs such as cartes de visite and cabinet cards were extremely common. These photos were printed on paper and were often classified according to the emulsion material (the top layer of the photo containing the image), such as albumen prints, salt prints, and so on. The photos came in various sizes and were mounted on a stiffer paper or cardboard, often imprinted with the photographer's name at the bottom.

Tintypes • The tintype was popular from the 1850's to the early 1900's (especially during the Civil War) because it was so inexpensive compared to earlier methods. Tintype photos, which tend to be dark, were printed on thin iron or tin plates and were sometimes mounted on cards.

MODERN PHOTOS

By the turn of the century, photography methods had become more standardized and photographs were increasingly common. Today, photographs can be categorized into three basic groups:

Instant Photos • Instant photographs (made popular by Polaroid)

are processed immediately so no negatives are involved. The chemicals used for developing are sealed in a packet with the photo. Instant photos generally fade very quickly, and they should never be cut (which would release the sealed chemicals).

Black-and-White Photos • By far the longest-lasting photographs are black and white. Older black-and-white photographs often have a white border around them and many are printed on fiber-based paper. The newer photos are printed on resin-coated paper, although some labs will, for a high price, still print on fiber-based paper.

Color Photos • Advances in color film have made today's color snapshots bright and sharp. However, any color photograph will fade over time because it is processed with dyes rather than the silver deposits used with black-and-white photos. (If you have color photographs from the 1950's or 60's, they have probably already started to fade.) Consider having black-and-white prints made of your most important color photos to preserve them even longer. And—for variety—don't forget to snap a roll of black-and-white pictures every once in a while.

DAMAGE AND REPAIR

Several factors determine how long a photograph will last: how it was originally processed, how it is handled, and how it is stored or displayed. Common deterioration problems include fading, yellowing, and cracking. Inadequate

card-mounted photos

processing can cause a photo to fade or become discolored over time. While you can't change how older photos were developed, you can shop around and try to find the best processing for the photos you're taking today.

A simple way to preserve an older photo is to have a copy made at a quality photographic lab (this is usually done by taking a picture of the photo). In addition to the new print, you'll also receive a negative for making future copies. Another option is to have the photograph electronically scanned, resulting in a digital format. Try to avoid photocopying older prints because the intense heat from the copier can accelerate deterioration. If an older photo has been damaged, don't try to repair it yourself, since there is as much potential for harm as for good. If the photo is especially significant, consider taking it to a photo preservation specialist.

TAKING CARE OF YOUR PHOTOS

Caring for older photographs is much the same as caring for newer ones. Several things can accelerate the deterioration of photographs, so proper handling and storage are necessary if you want to extend the life of a photo. Here are a few guidelines:

- Find a cool, dark storage location. High temperatures, high humidity, and bright light are all very harmful to photographs. Never store your photos in an attic, garage, or basement where the temperature and humidity levels can fluctuate greatly. The ideal storage condition is around 68° F with 50% humidity. You might want to consider storing your most valuable photographs in a safe-deposit box, which has a controlled environment.

- Watch out for insects (which are often attracted to the materials used in photographs) and damaging environmental elements such as air pollution, fumes from paint or cleaning agents, and salty sea air.

- Wash your hands before handling photographs and negatives, and wear cotton gloves if possible (especially with older photographs). Hold the photos with both hands by the edges to avoid fingerprints and cracking.

- Don't store your photographs with staples, paper clips, rubber bands, tape, or the like. These items can scratch your photos, emit harmful fumes, and accelerate chemical reactions within the photos.

- To help prevent pictures or negatives from sticking to each other, separate them with pieces of acid-free paper or store them in individual acid-free envelopes.

tintype

- If you have glass negatives, wrap them individually in acid-free paper and store them in small boxes.

- Store photographs in acid-free envelopes, file folders, boxes, or albums. Avoid wood boxes, and make sure any cardboard is acid-free. (You can test it with a pH testing pen as explained on page 33.)

- If you choose to display a favorite photograph, consider making a copy for framing and storing the original in a safe location. Mount the framed photo in a location away from direct sunlight or other bright lights, which can cause significant fading. For the frame, you can also use special Plexiglas that filters out ultraviolet radiation. A framed photograph should have a mat behind the photo for support and a mat in front of the photo to keep the print from touching the glass. (Be careful of the corrugated-cardboard backing that comes with many frames, since it can be highly acidic.)

Taking good care of your photographs—no matter when they were taken—is the best thing you can do to ensure that they'll be around long after you are!

• • • • Letters, Certificates, and Documents • • • •

IMAGINE YOUR excitement at discovering a stack of love letters written from a soldier to his sweetheart during a war. Or coming across the floor plan to your grandparents' first home. Simple pieces of paper such as these can be priceless treasures—especially when they're preserved in a scrapbook with accompanying photos and journaling. However, just like photographs, paper documents are fragile and must be handled and stored with great care to keep them in the best possible conditions and prevent deterioration.

Many documents—both old and new—are worth preserving. At the top of the list would be formal documents, such as birth, wedding, and death certificates, diplomas, and passports. Other awards, certificates, contracts, deeds, and report cards are also valuable records. Newspaper clippings and magazine articles featuring family members have always been scrapbook favorites. And personalities from any time period really shine through in handwritten letters, special school assignments, and art projects. (For more ideas on the types of things you can save for your scrapbook, see page 22.)

STORING DOCUMENTS SAFELY

Taking care of your important documents and letters to prevent deterioration is very similar to taking care of photographs. Follow these guidelines to help your documents stay in good condition:

- Avoid heat and high humidity, which can accelerate deterioration of the paper fibers and cause paper to become brown and brittle. Try to store important papers in a cool, dry location where the humidity level is constant.

- Store documents out of bright light, which causes ink to fade. And keep documents away from insects, food, dust, and harmful fumes.

- Consider keeping your most important documents and certificates in a safe-deposit box. The environmental conditions are good and they're protected from flood or fire damage.

- Place your documents in acid-free folders, boxes, or sheet protectors. You can also encapsulate documents in special polyester (Mylar) envelopes. Never laminate original documents, since the process cannot be reversed.

- Store pages flat if possible—folds weaken the fibers and are often the first place documents tear. If you have an older document that's folded, unfold it carefully, but don't force it.

- When storing multiple-page documents, place a sheet of acid-free, buffered paper between each page to help prevent acid migration. For documents stored in a folder, include a sheet of buffered paper at the front and back of the folder.

- If you have pages that have already started to deteriorate or that have a higher acid content, store them separately from other documents, and enclose them between two sheets of acid-free, buffered paper.

- Remove any rubber bands, paper

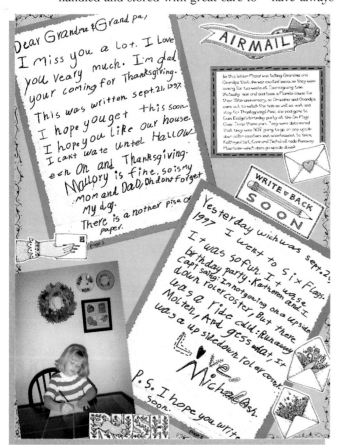

By Angela Ash, Lewisville, Texas. Scissors: Fiskars (Deckle); Stickers: Melissa Neufeld. The letters were photocopied onto acid-free paper and reduced to fit the layout.

What to Do with Newspaper Clippings

NEWSPAPER CLIPPINGS often make great additions to a scrapbook—birth and wedding announcements, obituaries, local articles featuring your family or your children's sports teams, and even stories about important national events. However, newspaper is usually the first type of paper to turn yellow and brittle, since it contains a high degree of acid. In addition, the acid from newspaper can travel to other documents or photos, causing them to deteriorate more rapidly. Here are a few suggestions for working with newspaper:

- Make a photocopy of the newspaper article on acid-free, buffered paper. Cream- or gray-colored paper might give the clipping a more authentic look. The photocopy can then be safely included in your scrapbook.

- Don't forget to record the title and date of the newspaper where the article appeared, either by writing them on the photocopy in permanent ink or by copying the newspaper masthead for that issue.

- If you want to store the original clipping, spray it with a deacidification spray, mount it on buffered paper with a water-based glue stick, and place it in a sheet protector. Periodically replace the buffered sheet with a new one. Store the clipping separately from any other documents or photos to prevent acid migration.

clips, and staples from documents. If the staples or paper clips are old and rusting, slide a thin piece of stiff plastic under the fastener on both sides of the page to protect the paper from tearing. Then, slide off the paper clip or use tweezers to bend the staple points and remove it.

- Never fix existing rips or tears with tape, which usually contains acid and can leave a gooey mess. It's best just to leave the document as it is and try to store it so it doesn't tear further. If the tear is particularly bad, you might take the document to a professional conservationist for repair.

INCLUDING DOCUMENTS IN A SCRAPBOOK

Letters, certificates, and other documents can help tell the story behind the photos in a scrapbook and reveal the personalities and unique talents of the people pictured. One of the safest ways to include an important document in your scrapbook is to copy the original onto acid-free paper. This allows you to store the original safely, using the guidelines above, yet still enjoy the document in your scrapbook.

Copying a document also gives you the flexibility of reducing it to fit easily on the scrapbook page. You can use a copied document as your entire page background or crop sections of it to include in various locations on the page. And don't forget that you can also make *color* copies to recapture the full beauty of an original document. (This works especially well for children's artwork.)

If you'd rather include the original document right in your scrapbook, place it on an acid-free, buffered page in a sheet protector, or encapsulate it in a clear Mylar envelope. You can also use a deacidification spray on the original before placing it in a sheet protector or envelope; this helps neutralize existing acids in the paper and keeps the paper from turning yellow and brittle. While this spray is not a permanent solution, it does help slow down the future development of acids. (Never use deacidification spray on photographs.) Be careful with newspaper, which is one of the most acidic forms of paper.

If the document is especially important or valuable, consider mounting it with photo corners so you don't alter the original and can easily remove the document later if needed.

Documents and letters of both yesterday and today can greatly enrich your scrapbook. Save unique documents that might help tell a story or reveal a personality. Then, take special care of those documents so they can be enjoyed for a lifetime—or longer!

• • • • Including Memorabilia in Scrapbooks • • • •

HOW MANY TIMES have you saved a memento from a special event only to rediscover it months (or years) later crushed in the bottom of a drawer? Even if you do carefully save keepsakes in an envelope or box, you probably don't get them out very often to enjoy them. On the other hand, scrapbooks *do* get pulled out frequently with the simple purpose of reminiscing and enjoying the memories. By safely including memorabilia items in your scrapbook pages, they too can be treasured again and again. (For ideas on the kinds of things you can collect, see "Memorabilia" on page 22.)

SAFE SCRAPBOOK MEMORABILIA

Memorabilia can enliven and enhance your scrapbook pages, but you need to be careful that the mementos you include won't harm the photographs or other important documents. So what items are safe for a scrapbook? In a nutshell, any item that is acid-free (or virtually acid-free) as well as relatively flat and smooth-edged can safely be affixed to a scrapbook page. If you're not sure whether a paper item is acid-free, you can easily test it with a pH testing pen. But don't despair if you have memorabilia that *don't* meet these requirements. Here are several other options for including in your scrapbook mementos that might contain acid or that aren't flat:

Photocopies • Make a color copy or photocopy of the item on acid-free paper. This works well for letters, chil-

dren's artwork, and paper documents with a high acid content, such as newspaper clippings or certain ticket stubs. Copying an item also allows you to reduce it if necessary to fit on the scrapbook page.

Deacidification Spray • You can preserve some paper items by using a deacidification spray and then mounting them on acid-free, buffered paper (see "Letters, Certificates, and Documents" on page 30 for more information).

Laminate • If the item is fairly flat, you can protect it with acid-free laminate or clear contact paper. Lamination works great for preserving pressed flowers and leaves, locks of hair, and other materials that might otherwise make a mess in your scrapbook (or even grow moldy). However, since lamination is nonreversible, you should never laminate something that you might want to use at a later date. Make sure you use acid-free laminate or contact paper, which can be purchased in self-adhesive sheets or rolls, or applied with a machine. If you want to include flowers or leaves, press them first for a week or two, using blotting paper to remove the moisture. You can use a flower press (two blocks of wood held together with screws and wing nuts and tightened a little every few days), or simply place the flowers and blotting paper in a large, heavy book. To be safe, seal dried flowers in laminate.

Plastic-Case and Shadow-Box Pages • Smaller mementos that

aren't flat enough to laminate can be displayed and protected using a scrapbook page designed for three-dimensional objects. These acid-free pages work great for displaying items such as seashells, jewelry, dried boutonnieres, coins, and so on. They can be found at scrapbook or craft stores and come in two basic types. Plastic-case pages include four to six different-sized trays (approximately 0.5" deep), with a backing that snaps into place. These pages are hole-punched for three-ring binders and come in two sizes: 8.5" x 11" and 12" x 12". Shadow-box pages have a sturdy pop-up window (about 0.25" deep) that's protected with clear Mylar. These pages are often decorated for a specific theme, such as weddings or new babies, and can be attached directly to your scrapbook page.

Photographs • If a memento is too large to include in your scrapbook, such as a trophy or quilt, take some photographs of it and the people associated with it. Then, journal the story of the item on the scrapbook page with the photos (and safely store the item separately). Photographs are also a great way to showcase a large collection if you're only able to include one or two actual items in the scrapbook.

IDEAS FOR USING MEMORABILIA

Once you've made sure your memorabilia are safe and protected, there are

By Channa Brewer, Mesa, Arizona. Background paper: The Paper Patch; Stickers: Sandylion.

lots of fun ways you can incorporate these items in your scrapbook. Here are just a few ideas:

- Use paper items (or color copies) for your page background or as decorations on the page. For example, use a map, travel brochure, or piece of artwork as the background for a page containing photos about the event. Or, cut a brochure or drawing into different shapes to position around the page.

- Attach the item directly on the page to create a border, frame a photo, or simply help tell the story. Many items can easily be attached to a page with photo splits (even things like baby socks), and you can also use acid-free glue sticks to keep things in place.

- Create a pocket page, which allows you to include items such as certificates and hospital bracelets. Simply place the loose items in the pocket and decorate the front as you would

any other scrapbook page. For more information on creating pocket pages, see page 78.

- You can also place keepsake items that you don't want to attach to a scrapbook page in their own sheet protector and insert this in your

album like a regular page. Or, use a plastic-case or shadow-box page as described above.

Don't let your memorabilia get buried in a box in your closet. Instead, enjoy them often by safely preserving them in your scrapbook!

Acid-Tester Pens

WHEN YOU'RE NOT SURE whether a paper item is acid-free and safe to use in your scrapbook, you can test it with a pH testing pen. These pens can be found at many scrapbook and craft stores and give you an easy way to test the acid content of a paper item, such as a ticket stub, program, sticker, or doily. (Unfortunately, there's no easy way to determine the acid content of nonpaper items, unless you're familiar with the exact materials and manufacturing process.)

To use a pH testing pen, simply draw a short line on the back of the item or in a

concealed location. Observe the color of the line as it dries to determine whether there is any acid in the paper. The chemicals in different pens turn different colors to indicate acid, so refer to the instructions with your specific pen to get the correct results.

It's also important to remember that pH testing pens are a somewhat informal test and aren't always 100% accurate. If you want to know the exact pH level of a product, contact the manufacturing company and request the results of its tests and research.

REXY - WHAT A CHARM

ABBY - KNOWS HOW

TO RELAX.

Materials AND Techniques

Learn fun ways to use scrapbooking tools and techniques

Several years ago the first scrapbook store opened in my neck of the woods, and I took an "all-night scrapbook madness" class. An instructor was on hand to help design pages. While I was excited to receive coaching on my scrapbook blueprints, I was even more eager to pick the teacher's brain about how to use all the neat supplies in the store.

This section is dedicated to satisfying your curiosity about the different ways to use scrapbooking supplies—including binders, pens, papers, stickers, die cuts, templates, software, and rubber stamps. It also goes a step further in helping you design better pages using a variety of these tools and creative techniques. Not only that, it addresses photo taking and photo journaling—taking better pictures and writing details that can make your scrapbook a personalized storybook. Read on, and have fun experimenting!

By Angelyn Bryce. Paper: The Paper Patch (polka dots); Scissors: Fiskars (Deckle); Die Cuts: Ellison; Palm tree: Angelyn's own design. (See Index for complete spread.)

4

Your Scrapbook

• • • • • • • • • • • • Large Binders • • • • • • • • • • • •

IT'S ONE OF THE first things you notice about a scrapbook, and it's also one of the first decisions you need to make when creating a scrapbook—the type of binder. Binders come in a huge variety of styles, colors, and sizes. They not only hold all of your scrapbook pages together but they keep them organized and protect their contents at the same time. Generally, larger binders (those that hold pages at least 8.5″ x 11″) are the choice for "main" scrapbooks, while smaller binders work well as gifts and specialty albums (see page 38).

There are three major styles of binders used for scrapbooks: three-ring binders, expandable-spine albums, and spiral-bound albums. Each style comes in an array of different sizes and colors, and each has benefits and drawbacks. By determining which features are most important to you, you can select the best binder for your scrapbook.

THREE-RING BINDERS

In a three-ring binder scrapbook, pages are created on paper or card-stock sheets and then placed in plastic sheet protectors. The protectors have punched holes for inserting the pages in the binder, and they serve to keep away dust, dirty fingers, and other harmful elements. Most three-ring binders hold 8.5″ x 11″ sheets, but you can also find half-size binders that hold 5.5″ x 8.5″ pages, as well as extra-large binders that hold 12″ x 12″ pages.

When you're shopping for a three-ring binder, look for one with D-shaped rings (instead of completely round O rings) so the pages will lie flat when the binder is closed. Also, select a binder that's slightly larger than the sheet protectors so the pages don't extend beyond the edge of the cover.

Pros • One of the biggest advantages of using a three-ring binder is its flexibility. It's easy to add and remove pages, as well as rearrange the page order. You're also free to use different background colors for the pages, and it's possible to photocopy or print clip-art images, text, borders, and embellishments directly on the scrapbook pages. In addition, you'll find a large selection of binder colors and cover types—from padded vinyl to tapestry tied with satin ribbons to canvas that can be drawn on or painted. The widest variety of patterned, colored, and textured papers is available for the 8.5″ x 11″ size. And, as a general rule, the supplies needed for a three-ring binder are less expensive than those needed for other types of binders.

Cons • Three-ring binders have several drawbacks. First, the smaller pages hold fewer pictures than do other types of albums. Second, if you want to create a two-page spread, the binder rings separating the facing pages break up the page continuity. Third, sheet protectors make it difficult to include pop-ups or pocket pages in your album. And finally, since pages can easily be removed, there is the possibility of lost or misplaced pages.

EXPANDABLE-SPINE ALBUMS

In an expandable-spine album, scrapbook pages are secured within the actual binding of the album. Many of these albums use a flex-hinge binding system, where pages are held in place by small wire loops (or staples) attached to the edge of each page. This allows the pages to lie completely flat when the album is opened, and also removes the gap between facing pages. Other albums use post hinges for the binding, where the pages are hole-punched to fit over the posts and don't generally lie flat.

Expandable-spine albums are

It's easy to make a simple spread with 8½″ x 11″ paper. By Jenica Lang, Las Vegas, Nevada. Pens: Zig Clean Color, Gelly Roll; Scissors: Fiskars (Cloud, Scallop); Other: NT Cutter.

usually the largest albums, with the most common size being 12″ x 12″. (Other available sizes include 8″ x 10″, 11″ x 14″, and 12″ x 15″.) These albums come filled with pages of a single color (usually white) and allow you to add and remove pages if needed. You can purchase different accessories for the album, such as page protectors, pocket pages, and specialty pages like lined journal pages and baby-album pages.

Pros • One of the things scrapbookers like most about expandable-spine albums is the ability to fit more photos and journaling on each page due to the larger size. In addition, two-page spreads work well because the facing pages are flush—allowing you to carry a title or other page element easily from one side to the other. And, since the pages are not in sheet protectors, pop-ups and pocket pages are readily created and enjoyed.

Cons • Expandable-spine albums are designed to carry photos and journaling on both sides of each page, but this can make it difficult to add pictures later or rearrange pages and still keep everything in the correct order. (It's also time-consuming to take apart the binding to add or remove pages.) In addition, the majority of patterned papers available aren't large enough to fit an entire page, although some suppliers do make decorative 12″ x 12″ pages. Other disadvantages of expandable-spine albums include: not being able to photocopy

A 12″ x 12″ page can be divided into a quilt-like pattern of nine perfect squares. By Karla Vos, Bellflower, California. Paper: Keeping Memories Alive, Canson, Creative Memories; Pens: Zig Clean Color; Die Cuts: Creative Memories.

or print directly on a page; always having the same background color (usually white); and the possibility of bindings breaking from the strain of a full album. *Note:* some expandable-spine albums now come with sheet protectors, instead of the actual album pages, held in the binding.

SPIRAL-BOUND ALBUMS

The third style of binder used for scrapbooks is a spiral-bound album, where the pages are permanently attached through a continuous wire coil that's the same length as the binder. Like other albums, spiral-bound albums come in a wide variety of sizes, including 8″ x 6″, 10″ x 10″, and 14″ x 14″. The pages are usually all the same color, the common options being white, black, and beige. Look for albums with sturdy, acid-free pages and strong bindings.

Pros • Spiral-bound albums are simple and easy to use, and they can result in some of the most beautiful and elegant

albums. The pages lie flat and give you a very consistent look and feel, making two-page spreads turn out nicely. You can easily include pop-ups and pocket pages because there are no sheet protectors. And, you can often personalize the album cover by drawing, painting, stamping, and using other decorations.

Cons • One downside of spiral-bound albums is that you can't add or rearrange pages because the binding is permanent (although for some types of albums, a permanent binding might be preferable). Another drawback is that there are currently no sheet protectors available that fit these albums. In addition, if a page is accidentally torn out, there's no way to replace it (without moving the pictures to a new page).

As you're deciding which type of binder to use for your scrapbook, remember that no one style is the best! It really comes down to which style suits *you* and your personality.

• • • • • • • • • • • • • • • Small Binders • • • • • • • • • • • • • •

WHEN YOU HEAR the word *scrapbook*, you might think of a large family album that's loaded with pictures and mementos from years past. But sometimes a full-sized binder is just too big for the scrapbook subject you have in mind. Smaller binders are ideal for specialty scrapbooks and gifts, and with several different styles to choose from, you're sure to find one that will spark ideas and suit your particular project's needs.

TYPES OF SMALL BINDERS

You can find smaller binders in each of the three main scrapbook styles: three-ring binder, spiral-bound album, and expandable-spine album. Each style has a distinctive look and feel, and each offers its own benefits. (For a more complete description of each binder style, see page 36.)

Three-Ring Binders • The smaller three-ring binders conveniently hold

5.5″ x 8.5″ pages (exactly half the size of 8.5″ x 11″ paper), so it's easy to use standard 8.5″ x 11″ cardstock by simply cutting it in half with a paper trimmer. (You can also purchase 5.5″ x 8.5″ cardstock from some suppliers.) Half-sized sheet protectors are also available.

Spiral-Bound Albums • Small spiral-bound albums are available in a 7″ x 10″ size. Their permanent binding, high-quality paper, and elegant proportions make them a perfect choice for gifts and specialty albums. Spiral-bound albums are relatively inexpensive and easy to use since they come with colored or textured paper already included.

Expandable-Spine Albums • It's possible to find expandable-spine albums in an 8″ x 10″ or 8″ x 6″ size, if you prefer this binding type. Pages can be added and removed as needed and are designed for you to add photos and text to both sides.

IDEAS FOR USING SMALL BINDERS

Smaller binders can be the perfect solution if you want to have only one or two pictures on each page without all of the extra space, or if you want to

create a special, easy-to-handle album for a child. Here are just a few ideas for albums you can create using a small binder:

ABC Books • ABC books are a great way to personalize the alphabet for a child (and use up your duplicate prints). For each letter of the alphabet, create one or two pages containing appropriate photos, die cuts, and stickers. If you're creating two pages per letter, use facing rather than back-to-back pages. Place a large letter on the page (it can be a die cut, stencil, sticker, or simply a handwritten letter) and label each of the related items on

A page from a small three-ring binder. By Becky Higgins, Peoria, Arizona. Die-cut leaves: Ellison.

the page. If you're creating the book for a specific child, try to use photos of that child wherever possible. For example, a page for the letter B might have photos of the child celebrating a birthday, playing with a brother, and swinging a baseball bat, along with die cuts or stickers of B objects, such as boats, barns, and books. You can also create "counting" scrapbook pages to help a child learn numbers.

Kids' Albums • Small binders are a great way for kids to get started creating their own scrapbooks. The smaller page size is less intimidating, and kids will love being able to decorate their own pages. Also, you'll get good use out of your duplicate photos.

School Albums • You can keep a fun record of the school years by creating a mini school album. Use two facing pages in a small binder to create a spread for each school year. Mount a 5" x 7" school picture on one side, and on the other side have the student write memories from that particular year. (See page 44 for some ideas on creating larger, more comprehensive school albums.)

"I Love You" Books • You can share your special memories with someone by creating a small "I Love You"

A spread from the same 5.5″ x 8.5″ album. By Becky Higgins, Peoria, Arizona. Die-cut leaves: Ellison.

album. Include a list of 50 (or more) reasons why you love that person — memories, qualities, talents, and so on. Then, add photos, die cuts, stickers, and other decorations to complement the reasons and top off the pages. If you're creating the album for a person who's a parent (it makes a great Mother's Day or Father's Day gift), you might allot several pages to each child to fill out the book.

Special-Day Albums • If you want to create a theme album for a holiday or other special event but don't have an awful lot of photographs, consider using a small binder. For example, you

might create a small album to highlight all of your family's Christmas celebrations over the years. Or, you might have a small binder devoted to photos from birthday celebrations. (For more ideas on creating theme albums, see page 42.)

When you're organizing the majority of your photographs into a scrapbook, a large binder is your best option. But if you want to showcase just a few photos or create a memorable gift, consider using one of the many small binders available. Their cozy appeal is sure to capture the hearts of all who pick them up.

• • • • • • • • • • Chronological Albums • • • • • • • • •

IT SEEMS NATURAL to organize scrapbooks in chronological order—after all, a scrapbook is a kind of personalized history book, and history is usually recounted in chronological order. By arranging photographs and memorabilia in order from past to present, we're better able to see the progressions that take place and to follow the stories being told through the pictures. Imagine thumbing through an album in which the photos had no order. Jumping back and forth between years every time you turned a page would be confusing, and if the photos weren't labeled, it would be even more difficult to identify the people and the time period.

HOW TO MAKE A CHRONOLOGICAL ALBUM

Here are a few basics you can follow to help in the process of creating a chronological album:

Organize Your Photos • Before you start working on your scrapbook, organize all of the photos that you want to include in the album in chronological order. Taking the time initially to organize your photos not only makes the scrapbooking process faster, it also ensures that you don't inadvertently leave out any pictures as you're creating the pages. You'll find additional tips on organizing your photos on page 18.

Pick a Starting Point • Once your photos are organized, you're ready to begin putting together your album. Decide which point in time you want to start creating pages for. If you're work-ing with a three-ring or expandable-spine album, you don't have to start with your oldest photos, even though those pages will eventually be at the beginning of your album. You might find it easier to start with the more recent photos and then gradually work back through the older photos. By working this way, you're able to remember more details about the newer photos while the memories are still fresh, and you'll have a greater sense of accomplishment at the same time.

For example, if you've got piles of photos from the past ten years to place in an album, you might start creating scrapbook pages with the photos from January of only one or two years ago. Then, after working forward through your pictures until you've caught up to the present, you can go back and do a year at a time of the older photos. Work at your own pace!

Select Photos for the Current Page • When you start working on a new scrapbook page, pull out the photos from the point where you left off. For example, if the last page you created had your Valentine's Day photos, find your pictures from spring of that same year. (This is where organization pays off.) Then, decide which individual photos you want to include on the same page. These might all be from the same event or holiday, or they might simply be seasonal snapshots, such as summer or winter activities. Of course, you can use more than one scrapbook page if

From 1984, by Linda Cottrell, Johnston, Iowa. Pens: Zig Clean Color; Scissors: Family Treasures (Deckle, Scallop); Computer Font: Inspirations (D.J. Twirl).

From 1985, by Linda Cottrell, Johnston, Iowa. Pens: Zig Clean Color; Scissors: Fiskars (Scallop); Die Cuts: Ellison; Computer Font: Fontastic! (D.J. Fatchat).

From 1986, by Linda Cottrell, Johnston, Iowa. Pens: Zig Clean Color; Scissors: Fiskars (Scallop); Clip art: "Copy Clip-n-Color Country Creations" by Annette Ward; Hat: Linda's own design.

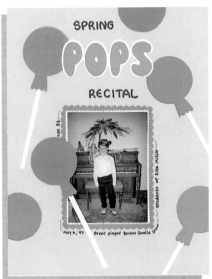

From 1993, by Linda Cottrell, Johnston, Iowa. Pens: Zig Clean Color; Scissors: Fiskars (Scallop, Mini-Scallop); Pops: Linda's own design.

you have a lot of photos from the same event.

For those miscellaneous or everyday shots, you might want to group together photos that date within a few months of each other but share a similar theme, such as children playing dress-up or the adventures of your new pet. However, to help keep the chronological flow of your album, try not to span too large a time frame on the same page. And remember that you don't have to use every picture in your scrapbook.

Date the Page • Finally, remember to note the date somewhere on each page—at least the month and year. Even though it might be obvious to *you* when the photos were taken, others who look at your album (especially in the future) won't have that advantage. And if the page becomes separated from the album, you'll know exactly where it belongs. There are lots of ways to include the date. You can make it part of the page title, or, if you don't want it to be too intrusive,

simply note it in fine print in a page corner. If the pictures on the page aren't all from the same date, you can indicate the date underneath or alongside each photo. (For more ideas on journaling in your scrapbook, see the sections beginning on page 120.)

CHRONOLOGICAL VS. THEME ALBUMS

Even though creating scrapbooks in chronological order is a popular choice, it's not the only option. One alternative is a theme album, which includes only those pictures that relate to a specific event, rather than all of your pictures in continuous chronological order. Chronological albums work well for general albums and especially for baby albums, because of all the "firsts" that occur in the early years of life. Theme albums work better for events that occur on a regular basis, such as holidays, vacations, and birthdays.

However, even in a theme album, the pictures are still usually organized in chronological order. For example, if you create a Christmas album, you'll probably organize the pictures accord-

ing to year. And, of course, you can create *both* chronological and theme albums. For example, you might organize the general family scrapbook in chronological order but also have a special vacation album that contains only the family vacation pictures.

BENEFITS OF A CHRONOLOGICAL ALBUM

While theme albums work well for certain types of pictures, chronological albums also have several advantages:

- Your pictures are all in one place, so you don't have to keep track of different albums.
- You have a place to include those great but miscellaneous photos that wouldn't fit in a theme album.
- It's easy to organize and sort your photographs in chronological order—and keep your system updated as you take new pictures.
- You can enjoy watching the natural progression of people, especially children, throughout the years.
- If a page is removed from your album, you can easily reinsert it in the correct location, especially if the date is included somewhere on the page.

Creating a chronological scrapbook is a great way to present your photographs. Don't rule out creating a few special theme albums—these are also quite enjoyable—but by keeping the majority of your photos in order, your album will have a natural flow and will be an invaluable historical record at the same time.

• • • • • • • • • • • • • • Theme Albums • • • • • • • • • • • • • •

IN A CHRONOLOGICAL scrapbook, it can be difficult to make those extra-special events or holidays stand out. For a distinctive presentation, try creating a theme album. Theme albums contain only those pictures that relate to a specific topic, such as Christmas, vacations, or a school year. They're a wonderful way to capture the special spirit of those memorable occasions.

WHY CREATE A THEME ALBUM?

While it's a good idea to organize your main scrapbook in chronological order, that doesn't mean you can't also have one or two separate theme albums. There are several reasons why creating a theme album is worthwhile:

Speed and Satisfaction • Since each theme album involves a much smaller number of photographs (especially compared to the piles waiting for your regular album), you'll be able to get them into an album in a relatively short period of time. Not only will this give you a tremendous amount of satisfaction, it can also help keep you from getting discouraged by the slow pace of work on your other albums. You'll get caught up on your theme album quickly, and if the album

ask people to send notes and photos for a tribute album

is for an ongoing theme, you can easily update it when new pictures are developed.

Enjoyment • Theme albums are a fun way to see how styles, family members, and traditions have changed, especially when the pictures show several years' worth of the same event or holiday. Since there are usually only a handful of pages devoted to each year, you can see the changes simply by turning a few pages—and they're more dramatic than if you viewed them in a larger album.

Faster Setup and Cleanup • If you work on the same theme album for several consecutive scrapbooking sessions, you'll need to pull out only those supplies (paper, stickers, die cuts, and so

on) that relate to that theme. This can significantly reduce the amount of time you need for setup and cleanup, especially if you already have your supplies organized according to themes.

Easy Page Layouts • Theme albums can also help you work faster because you don't need new creative ideas for each new page. Instead, with the use of a consistent color scheme and similar design elements for each page in a particular year, there's no need to agonize over making each page unique. (You'll find more information about designing theme pages below.)

Star Treatment • Theme albums keep your extra-special photos from getting lost among your more ordinary ones, preserving more of their magic and charm.

HOW TO MAKE A THEME ALBUM

Putting together a theme album is a rewarding—and fun—experience. Here are a few guidelines to help you along:

Choose the Theme • First, you'll need to decide what type of album you want to create. Theme albums work great for annual events like holidays and family reunions, as well as for special one-time events, such as weddings or bar mitzvahs. If you're creating scrapbooks for children, you can also divide each individual album into several theme sections (birthdays, friends, outings, holidays, etc.).

Organize Your Photos • Having your photos organized greatly speeds up the process of creating any type of scrapbook. Sort your photographs according to the albums you want to create. For example, if you're creating a Christmas album, place all of your Christmas pictures together. (You might also want to further sort each group chronologically.) If you don't have photos for that event from one or two years, that's okay—try creating a journal page with your memories from that year. (For more ideas on organizing photos, see page 18.)

Create a Title Page • Each year or event in your album should have a title page to help identify and separate each group of pages. Select a photo for the title page that represents the event, such as a family photo in front of the Christmas tree, a school portrait, or a photo in front of a landmark visited on vacation. Include the year or event title in large letters, as well as any other pertinent information, such as the location. Use the same basic layout for each title page in your album (changing the color scheme perhaps), so you can easily find the beginning of each section.

Choose a Consistent Look • As you work on the pages for each year or event, make them distinctive somehow.

By Becky Higgins, Peoria, Arizona. Pens: Zig Writers, EK Success; Pencils: Prisma Color; Torn paper: Personal Stamp Exchange (green mulberry).

By Traci Folkersen, Sandy, Utah. Pens: Marvy Le Plume II; Stickers: R.A.Lang, Susan Winget; Corner rounder: Marvy Uchida.

have fun assembling the tribute album with family photos and other decorations

One of the best ways to do this is to use the same color scheme on each page within a year (including the title page). You can also connect the pages by using similar decorations, such as repeating a particular die cut, punch, or sticker style on each page, or using the same lettering style. Creating a consistent look for each year or event is pleasing to the eye and makes it easier to find the beginning and ending of each section.

Don't Forget the Memorabilia • Special events and holidays often have lots of fun memorabilia associated with them. Adding these items to your theme album along with the photographs can greatly enhance the pages. You might include school reports, artwork, change-of-address notices, announcement memos, party invitations, shopping lists, travel brochures, ticket stubs, and so on. (For more ideas on collecting memorabilia, see page 22.)

Place the Pages in a Unique Binder • To make your album really stand out, store the pages in a binder decorated to reflect the theme. The cover of the binder not only makes the album contents easy to recognize, it also adds to the overall spirit of the memories. You can create your own album cover with fabric or paint, or you can purchase an album that's suitable to the theme. (For more ideas on covering albums, see page 48.)

IDEAS FOR THEME ALBUMS

You can create a theme album for practically any occasion—here are a few ideas to get you started:

Christmas • The Christmas album is one of the most popular types of theme albums, since Christmas photos are usually abundant and easy to sort out from your other pictures. In addition to the traditional photos of trees and presents, try to include pictures that capture your family's traditions and unique celebrations, such as baking, caroling, decorating the house, and so on. Other items that make a great addition to a Christmas album include the family's yearly newsletter (if you send one), photos and cards from family and friends, and letters to Santa.

School • School albums are a nice way to record the achievements and activities that take place during a

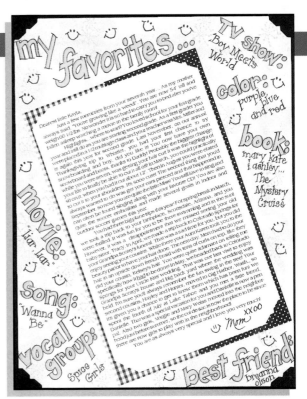

The theme of a birthday party can set the tone for scrapbook pages. Try posing a child as if she's holding a sign—then paste one on later. All by Marita Kovalik, Portland, Oregon. Paper: The Paper Patch (gingham and polka dot) and unknown (pillow ticking); Pens: Micron Pigma 005 and 05, Black and Yellow Ochre Tombow, Yellow Marvy; Scissors: Fiskars (Notch) and decoupage scissors; Rubber Stamps: "Picture Framed" and Ponytail's "Smiley-Face," D.O.T.S.; Other: black embossing powder, round sponge with yellow Marvy marker.

An annual letter from mom becomes one of the pages. Paper: The Paper Patch; Pen: Micron Pigma 005; Scissors: Fiskars (Notch); Font: Americana; Rubber Stamps: Ponytail's "Smiley Face" and Super Set's "Fireworks," D.O.T.S.; Other: round sponge with yellow Marvy marker.

Pen: Micron Pigma 005; Scissors: Fiskars (Notch); Rubber Stamps: Camera, "Picture Framed," Ponytail's "Smiley Face" and Super Set's "Fireworks," D.O.T.S.; Other: round sponge with yellow Marvy marker.

A pocket page helps keep birthday mementos safe. Paper: Memory Press (plaid); Pens: Micron Pigma 005, Yellow Ochre Tombow, Yellow Marvy; Scissors: Fiskars (Notch and Deckle) and decoupage scissors; Rubber Stamps: Ponytail's "Smiley Face," D.O.T.S.; Other: black embossing powder, round sponge with yellow Marvy marker; single hole punch and yellow ribbon.

a tribute album makes a heartfelt gift

school year. You can place all of a student's school photographs and mementos in a single album (with a title page separating each year), or you can create separate albums for each type of school, such as elementary, junior high, and high school. Some particularly busy years might even merit their very own album, such as a senior year in high school (for this year, it's neat to create a page showing all the school portraits from kindergarten to graduation). You can include artwork, report cards, autographs of friends and teachers, field-trip souvenirs, book reports, and so on. Don't forget to include a handwriting sample from each year, or have the student write memories on the actual scrapbook page. Children can even create their own school albums, which gives them a sense of accomplishment. And, if done jointly, it provides parent and child with valuable time together.

Vacation • If travel is an activity you enjoy, consider creating a vacation theme album. Every time you take a trip—whether it's an overnight camp-out or a two-week European tour—add a new section to your album with photos and memorabilia to record your adventures. (See page 22 for ideas on

things you can collect on your journeys.)

Family Reunion • Family reunions are a wonderful time for visiting, reminiscing, and participating in lively activities. If your family organizes reunions every year or so, keep all those memories together in a reunion theme album. You'll enjoy seeing how each family has grown and changed over the years, and the album can even do double duty in keeping track of your family's genealogy. Don't forget to take group photos of each family in attendance, and you might also have each family provide a written update of events that have occurred since the last reunion.

Wedding • A wedding album can be an elegant presentation of the excitement and celebration of a wedding day. You can create an album containing your own wedding pictures and mementos, or if you have married children, you can place photos from each wedding in the same album. (Begin each section with a large photo of the bride and groom.) You'll want to include photos of all the wedding activities—including bridal showers, rehearsals, and decorating the car—as well as memorabilia such as the invitation, an embossed napkin, or pressed flowers.

Tribute Albums • If you're looking for a unique and personalized way to honor an important person, consider creating a tribute album. This type of

Kids love to see themselves in an ABC album. By Karen Van Hatcher, Tigard, Oregon. Scissors: Fiskars (Stamp); Stickers: Mrs. Grossman's; Sticker Letters and Die Cuts: Creative Memories.

album is especially nice for milestone events, such as a 50th wedding anniversary, retirement, graduation, or special birthday. To create a tribute album, send small index cards to people who have been influenced by the person you're honoring, such as family members and friends. Have them write "tributes" on the cards, mentioning qualities they admire or favorite memories they have of the person, and then return the cards to you along with a photograph if possible. Then, on each page of a small album (spiral-bound albums work well), mount the photographs and corresponding cards, adding other decorations if you want. These albums are sure to be treasured gifts!

Anniversary • An anniversary album can be a wonderful tribute to your married life together. You might start the album with a few wedding photos, and then include a photo of you and your spouse each year, along with a photo of your home at the time and information about jobs, children, pets, and so on. Anniversary theme albums can also commemorate milestones such as 10th, 25th, or 50th anniversary celebrations.

Baby • Mothers have been putting together baby books for generations. These albums help preserve all the important firsts that accompany the arrival of a new family member. Some baby albums cover only the first year of life, while others include memories from the first three or four years. Items commonly kept in a baby album include birth announcements, letters written by the parents right after the birth, hospital bracelets, handprints and footprints, a record of height and weight changes, and, of course, lots and lots of photos. You can also purchase baby-album pages designed to help you record pertinent data.

Other Ideas • The possibilities for creating a theme album are limited only by your imagination (and the types of photos you have). Some other theme album ideas include birthdays, holidays other than Christmas (such as the Fourth of July, Thanksgiving, and New Year's), ABC albums (see page 38), military service, and an album for grandparents.

Theme albums are an ideal way to preserve and display photos and memorabilia from special holidays and events. If you decide to create a theme album, remember to stick with your organization and keep all of the related photos together. (If you're tempted to put a photo in one of your other albums, make sure you get a duplicate made.) Your album will be more enjoyable to view with everything in one place—and you'll enjoy the ease of keeping it up to date!

Scrapbooks as Gifts

THE BEST GIFTS ARE THOSE that come from the heart—gifts that have been tailored with love for the unique interests and personality of the recipients. That's why scrapbooks make such wonderful gifts—and there are so many possibilities too! You can give a completed scrapbook or only a binder with a few pages created and a promise to add more pages throughout the year. Another option is to give a binder with either blank pages or decorated pages containing everything but the photos and captions.

Here are a couple of ideas for scrapbooks that make great gifts (see pages 38 and 39 for several other ideas):

Grandparents' Album • What grandparent doesn't love to show off photos of the grandchildren? Scrapbooks are an ideal way to display and preserve those precious pictures. Have the grandkids help personalize the pages with drawings or comments. (If they're too young to write, have them dictate their thoughts about their grandparents to you.) Larger photos can be held in place with photo corners, so they can also be displayed for a time in a frame if desired. And don't forget to keep the album updated with new pages as the grandchildren grow.

Grandbaby Journal • If there's a new grandchild in the family, grandparents can put together a first-year journal that's sure to be appreciated by busy new parents. Keep track of such things as vital statistics, funny anecdotes, special visits, nicknames, and all those "firsts." If you can keep the journal a surprise, that's even better!

• • • • • • • • • Making Covers and Labels • • • • • • • •

WHILE SCRAPBOOKING focuses mainly on creating pages that go inside an album, don't forget that you can add a little personality to the outside of your album as well. Some purchased albums already have beautiful covers in materials such as tapestry, padded vinyl, and buckram, which often need no further embellishments. But many binders are perfect for customizing—and you can have a lot of fun doing so!

PERSONALIZED ALBUM COVERS

An album cover can communicate a lot about its contents, especially if it's a theme album (see page 42). For example, a wedding album might be covered with beautiful white satin and lace, along with a framed photo of the bride and groom. Or, a school album might be decorated with the child's name and artwork. Chronological albums can also have fun covers and titles, from something as simple as "The Jones Family, 1991–1994" to something as elaborate as a patchwork quilt where each family member has decorated his or her own quilt square.

Several types of albums can easily be customized, including canvas, fabric, and spiral-bound albums. Here are some ideas for covering each type:

Canvas • Canvas-covered albums allow you to draw, paint, stamp, and stencil directly on the cover. Several different compa-

nies make canvas albums. The cover is usually white, but you can add a lot of color with different decorating techniques. (Ink sponging is a fast way to cover the entire album.) Be sure to use waterproof, permanent markers to draw on the cover.

Spiral-Bound • Like canvas albums, spiral-bound albums have covers that are perfect for personalizing. You can decorate the cover by drawing, stamping, gluing, and so on. You can easily personalize most spiral-bound albums using the same techniques and materials you use inside the scrapbook.

Fabric • With so many fabric patterns and styles available, the possibilities for fabric-covered albums are endless.

A handpainted wooden binder. By Jackie Morley, Las Vegas, Nevada. Wooden binder: Keepsake Kaddies; Pattern: Reed Baxter.

Many fabric and tapestry albums can be purchased premade in hundreds of patterns, including holidays, sports, florals, and much more. Or, you can easily create your own cover using a few pieces of fabric and any three-ring binder. (See instructions below.) Fabric covers are often padded for added beauty and texture, and many have ribbon ties or lace around the edges. One of the great things about a fabric cover is that you can add almost anything to it to further enhance your album, such as buttons, photos, and so on.

Three-Ring • Some three-ring binders have a clear, full-sized plastic pocket on the front cover that you can slip paper or photos into, making them a cinch to customize. With these binders, you could even use a regular scrapbook page as your album cover!

HOW TO MAKE A FABRIC COVER

Creating a fabric cover for a three-ring binder isn't as difficult as you might think. You can purchase a kit with an unassembled binder to which you affix your own material before attaching the rings. (The binder is coated with an adhesive.) Or, you can make your own using a very simple, no-sew method. This method also easily allows you to add padding, lace, and ribbon ties to a pre-existing three-ring binder. Follow these steps:

1. Lay a three-ring binder out flat and measure the full width and height. Add 1″ to both the width and height and cut a piece of fabric that

size for the outside. If you want to pad the cover, cut a piece of batting just slightly larger than the width and height of the entire binder.

2. Measure the width and height of the inside sections of the cover, from the edge to where the binder bends at the spine. If you have a D-ring binder, measure the back inside cover from the edge to the rings. Add 1″ to both the height and width and cut a piece of fabric for each side. (You can either use the same fabric as the outside or a contrasting color.)

3. Subtract ½″ from the width and height of each inside section you just measured and cut a piece of fairly thin cardboard for each size.

4. If you have an O-ring binder, cut two additional strips of inside fabric approximately 3″ wide and the same height as the binder. For a D-ring binder, measure the width of the spine and add 2″, then cut a strip of inside fabric this size (the same height as the binder). Cut a second strip approximately 2″ wide and the same height.

5. Using a fabric or craft glue, glue the two small strips of inside fabric along each side of the binder rings, tucking them slightly underneath the rings. For a D-ring binder, glue the wider strip in the front cover, so it also covers the spine.

6. Lay the outside fabric piece face-down, then center the batting and binder on top of the fabric. Apply glue along the inside edges of the binder (and over the small fabric strips) and pull the fabric over to glue it on the inside.

7. If you want to use lace or ribbon ties, glue them along the inside edge of the binder.

8. Lay the inside fabric pieces facedown and center the two cardboard sections over them. Glue the fabric around the edges of the cardboard as you did with the outside fabric.

9. Finally, glue the covered cardboard pieces (fabric-side up) in the center of each inside section of the binder, making sure the binder can close freely.

COVER EMBELLISHMENTS

Once you've got the basic cover on your binder, you can customize it even further by adding one or more embellishments. These decorations can be glued or sewn to the cover. Here are just a few ideas:

- Photos—you can even create a separate photo frame out of fabric or other materials
- Medals
- Scout badges
- Buttons
- Pockets
- Wood ornaments
- Ribbons, lace, raffia, etc.

LABELING YOUR BINDER

Finally, consider labeling your binder

A handmade wedding album cover. By Janet Merkley, Green River, Wyoming. Satin, lace, ribbon, and silk flowers on a padded cover.

with a title and date. Labels are especially useful for chronological albums, since you can tell at a glance which dates are covered in each binder. The label might simply include your family name and date, or it might be a more descriptive title, such as "Vacation Adventures" or "Christmas Memories." Many vinyl binders have a simple pocket on the spine where you can insert a cardstock label. Or, you can incorporate the title as part of your cover decorations.

Album covers can convey a lot about a scrapbook before the first page is even turned. Putting a little thought into the cover will give you an album with a lot of personality!

5

Design Basics

• • • • • • • • • • • • • Good Design • • • • • • • • • • • • • •

SOME SCRAPBOOK PAGES really catch your eye, while others can hardly coax a second glance. What's the difference? Often, the distinguishing characteristic between a great scrapbook page and a so-so page is the layout and design. Bright colors and flashy lettering don't guarantee a successful page. Instead, the best pages bring out the best in the photographs through the careful selection of colors, page accents, and so on. Even if you don't think you have a knack for design, you can improve your scrapbook pages by following a few simple design principles.

CHOOSE A THEME

Most scrapbook pages are built around a general theme, which can be anything from an elaborate holiday celebration to a simple afternoon walk. All of the photos on the page (as well as most of the accents) relate to the chosen theme in one way or another, tying the page together. One of the first steps in creating a page is to decide on your theme and the kind of feeling you want your page to convey.

Look through your photos and select those that would best fit together on a page. Depending on the size of your album pages and how much you crop the pictures, you'll usually be able to fit three to six photos on a page. If you have lots of photos from the same event, you might

want to create a two-page spread or even a series of storytelling pages.

Remember that you don't have to use *all* of your photos in your scrapbook. Instead, select the best photos—those that turned out great visually as well as those that hold special significance, even if the shot itself isn't perfect. (You can store the extra photos safely in an acid-free box.) Also, try to select a variety of different shots. For example, you might choose a group shot, several closeups, and an action shot. Or, you might have your pictures tell the story by including shots from the beginning, middle, and end of the event.

ARRANGE THE PAGE

Once you've selected the photos and

theme you want to work with, your next step is determining how you want to arrange the photos on the page. Here are a few guidelines:

Choose a Focal Point • Every page needs a focal point—somewhere for the eye to start. Choose one or two of your best photos to be the focus of your page. These are usually photos that are a good representation of the overall theme and require little (if any) cropping. You can help draw attention to these photos by placing them off-center on the top third of the page, mounting them on coordinating paper, or tilting them slightly.

Create Flow and Balance • The position of each photograph should contribute to the overall page flow, leading your eye from one picture to the next. By angling and overlapping photographs, you can help direct viewers through the layout from start to finish. Don't be afraid to extend one or two corners of a photo completely off the edge of the page and then trim the photo flush with the page. However, you don't need to angle or overlap every photograph on the page—in fact, you'll often make more of a visual impact by skewing just one or two. In addition, remember that the size, location, and angle of each photo should give the page a balanced feel.

Select Effective Shapes • Many

photos can be improved with careful cropping. Cropping helps focus on the subject of the photo by removing unnecessary details and also allows you to fit more photos on a page. Select shapes that will enhance your page theme and flow, and try not to use too many different shapes on the same page. Some of the most common and eye-pleasing shapes for cropping include rectangles, circles, and ovals.

Before actually mounting any photos on your page, lay them down and experiment with different positions and angles. By testing different arrangements, you'll be able to find one that brings out the best in your photographs and enhances the overall theme as well.

By Becky Higgins, Peoria, Arizona. Pens: Zig Writers, EK Success; Stickers: Mrs. Grossman's (basket); Main Street Press Ltd. (heart).

(And don't forget to leave room for journaling!)

SELECT A COMPLEMENTARY BACKGROUND

The colors that you choose for the page and photo backgrounds have a big impact on the mood of the page. Lay your photos over different colors of paper to see the different effects you can get. Select a few colors that coordinate with and accentuate the photos. For example, you wouldn't want to use hot and bright colors for pictures of an overcast, rainy vacation. For more tips on working with color, see "Design with Color Photos" on page 58.

In addition to colors, look for shapes, textures, and patterns from your photographs that you can repeat in the page background through accents and photo frames. Try to avoid having too many different colors and textures on a single page so the focus remains on the photos.

ADD ACCENTS TO ENHANCE

After mounting the photos on the page, you're ready to add the finishing touches. Accents such as stickers, die cuts, computer fonts, and stamped images can enhance your photos, fill in empty space, and strengthen your theme. But be careful that you don't go overboard. Having too many accents can result in a cluttered and distracting page—a common problem in scrapbooks.

Choose accents that support

By Becky Higgins, Peoria, Arizona. Torn paper: Personal Stamp Exchange (green mulberry); Punch: Family Treasures.

the look and feel you're trying to achieve with your page. Try to place coordinating stickers and die cuts that draw the eye, use decorative scissors with an appropriate edge, and add lettering that complements the page's shapes, colors, and mood. Always keep in mind that your goal is to enhance your photos, not distract from them.

Creating a well-designed scrapbook page is something that gets easier with practice. Look at other scrapbook pages and see what works well and what doesn't. Then try out some techniques in your own album. But at the same time, strive to develop your own unique style (see page 54), and remember that different people have different tastes. By paying attention to design elements such as focus, color, shape, and placement, you'll be able to create visually appealing pages that grab—and keep—attention.

• • • • • Keeping the Focus on the Photos • • • • •

WHEN YOU SIT DOWN to look through a scrapbook, you probably don't spend your time scrutinizing every sticker, color, or decorative-scissor edge used on the pages. Instead, you enjoy reminiscing over the *photographs* and the memories they evoke—the other elements on the page simply enhance this experience. That's why the best scrapbook pages are designed with carefully selected page layouts and accents that keep the main focus on the photos. Fortunately, there are lots of ways you can keep your photos at "center stage" in your scrapbook,

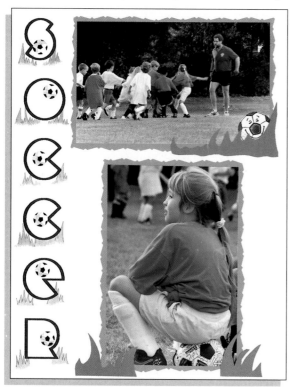

By Marita Kovalik, Portland, Oregon. Scissors: Fiskars (Bow Tie); Stickers: source unknown; Font: Shotfun; Grass: Marita's own design.

including photo selection, placement, frames, and embellishments.

TAKING AND SELECTING PHOTOS

One of the best ways to make pictures the focus in your scrapbook is to improve the photographs themselves. Here are a few guidelines for taking and selecting pictures that grab attention:

- Invest in a good camera and then practice using good photography techniques such as shooting at close range, paying attention to the background and lighting, and capturing a variety of shots. The better your photos are to begin with, the better your scrapbook page will be. (See the photography sections beginning on page 86 for more information.)

- Develop your film with a larger print size, such as 4" x 6". The larger photos stand out more on the page, show more detail, and allow you to crop without making the pictures too small.

- Select one or two good closeup photos for each scrapbook page, if possible. These pictures naturally draw your eye more than group

shots or medium-range shots. They also make great focal points, since they hold their own weight visually and usually don't need much cropping.

- Focus in on the subjects of your photos by carefully cropping out distracting details (see page 98 for tips on cropping). However, be careful that you don't crop *too* many pictures—try to keep at least one or two larger photos on the page to provide balance and serve as focal points. When a page is full of small, cropped photos, it's easy for them to get lost among the other page embellishments.

PHOTO PLACEMENT

The position of the photographs on each page can create a visual flow and direct your eye accordingly. Experiment with these different layout ideas to help keep the eye focused on the photos:

- Place your largest photos in the top left and bottom right corners of the page, with smaller ones positioned in between. Most people naturally scan a page this way (the result of reading), and this balanced layout directs the eye comfortably. Alternately, you can position the larger photos in the top right and bottom left corners. (This works especially well for right-hand pages.)

- If you have only one large photo, position it off-center somewhere in the top third of the page, then balance out the page with smaller photos in the lower section.

On this well-designed page, strong page accents don't upstage the photos. By Ellen James, Pleasant Grove, Utah. Paper: The Paper Patch; Stickers: Sandylion; Die Cut letters: Ellison; Stencil: Cloud, D.O.T.S.

- To help your main photo stand out, tilt it slightly toward the center of the page, leaving the rest of the photos in a horizontal position. Or, try placing the main photo horizontally and angling all of the others in its direction.

- Where possible, position your photos so that the subject faces either the center of the page or the main photo. When the subject in a picture is facing the edge of the page, the eye tends to follow right off the page!

- Overlap photos and use their shapes to help lead the eye from one photo to another.

PHOTO FRAMES

A popular—and effective—way to emphasize a photograph is to frame it. Framing is commonly done by mounting the photographs on coordinating colors of cardstock, but there are lots of other fun options as well. (See "Photo Mounting and Framing Options" on page 94 for ideas.) Choose a frame color or pattern that coordinates with the overall page theme and brings out a particular element in the photo. Experiment with multiple colors and different thicknesses to see what effects you can create. If you want a photo to really stand out, choose a frame color that contrasts (but doesn't clash with) the background page. (For more hints on designing pages for color photos, see page 58.)

PAGE ACCENTS

Page accents such as stickers, die cuts, stamped images, and borders can greatly enhance the photos on the page, but if you're not careful they can also be very distracting. Here are a few suggestions for using accents effectively:

- Choose accents that correspond to the photo content, page theme, and selected colors, and then use them judiciously to decorate your page.

- When positioning stickers and die cuts, face them toward a photo or the center of the page to direct your eye there.

- Try drawing in "movement" lines for appropriate stickers or die cuts

to lead the eye to a specific photo.

- Create a simple border around the entire page to help define the center area. You can create borders with a marker or by using stickers, stamped images, or clip-art programs.

Well-thought-out frames and other embellishments can make your photos shine on the page even more than they would on their own. With a little bit of planning, you can make your photographs the spotlight of every scrapbook page, helping you enjoy and relive your memories each time you open your album.

• • • • Developing and Expressing Your Style • • • •

A WONDERFUL THING about scrapbooking is that it's a unique expression of your own creativity and personal style. Given the exact same pictures, two people can put together very different-looking scrapbook pages. Even if the pages use a similar design and layout, they still might look quite distinct when it comes to the colors chosen, style of stickers, lettering technique, and so on.

Just as people have different tastes when it comes to decorating their homes or selecting their wardrobes, people have individual preferences for scrapbooking styles. There's no one right style, although there are some basic design princi-

A whimsical style. By Gwendy Kem, Scottsdale, Arizona. Paper: Creative Card; Scissors: Fiskars (Scallop and Pinking), Family Treasures (Jumbo Deckle); Stickers: Mrs. Grossman's; Die Cuts: Ellison; Fonts: D.J. Crayon, Fontastic!, D.J. Inkers.

ples that are always good to follow (see page 50). You can decide which style suits you best, or even use a variety of styles throughout your scrapbook.

SCRAPBOOKING STYLES
So what exactly is a "scrapbooking style"? The style sets the overall look and feel of a scrapbook page and can encompass everything from the colors to the photo shapes to the captions. While styles are as unique as the person doing the scrapbooking, many styles fit into a general category, such as those described below:

Bold • A modern look with bright colors and bold titles. The pages might use lots of geometric shapes, such as squares, circles, and triangles. Primary colors often predominate in page decorations and lettering.

Classic • A more traditional and formal look, with very little photo cropping and sparse use of page accents such as stickers and die cuts. Photo corners might be used for an old-fashioned feel, and an emphasis is placed on journaling names and dates. Common colors include black, white, cream, and navy.

Victorian • Pages with ornate floral and lace backgrounds, flowing script handwriting, and stickers and rubber stamps with a 19th-century feel. Deep colors, such as burgundy, are characteristic of this style.

Romantic • An elegant look that's reminiscent of a quieter, simpler time. These pages commonly use flowers, flowing lines, and rounded edges,

but they aren't as ornate as the Victorian style.

Whimsical • Pages that incorporate several stickers, clip-art images, hand-lettering techniques (or computer fonts), and other elements to create a cute and charming touch. These pages are often very theme-oriented with clever page titles and captions.

Country • A homespun look created from hand-drawn "stitching" and calico patterns. Common page accents include hearts, sunflowers, and teddy bears.

Child-Oriented • Pages created with fun elements that children would enjoy looking at, such as clowns, trains, and cartoon characters. Lots of bright colors are used, along with basic shapes.

Of course, not every scrapbook page fits neatly in a specific style category. Your style might simply be to create fun pages using a variety of colors and accents without necessarily focusing on an obvious theme or repeated motif.

FINDING YOUR STYLE
Finding a scrapbooking style that expresses your personality isn't always easy. For starters, think about your own tastes and the general style of pages you find most attractive. Use the following questions to help:

• What are your favorite colors? Do you prefer pastels, bright colors, or earth tones?

• When you're looking at stickers, clip-art images, or rubber stamps, what style do you usually select?

A bold, child-oriented style. By Mary Asay, Mesa, Arizona. Pens: Sakura Micron Pigma; Scissors: Fiskars (Bow Tie); Stickers: Mary Englebreit; Die Cuts: Ellison; Font: Microsoft Word (Franciscan); Punch: Punch Line (Mini-star).

- Do you have a favorite motif that you like to use for embellishing, such as hearts, stars, flowers, teddy bears, or cats? Do you live in an area that is associated with certain objects, such as the country (cows, barns), the mountains (pine trees), or the coast (seashells)?

- Is there a writing style—either your own handwriting or a computer font—that you find attractive and frequently use?

The answers to these questions often become the most defining aspects of the style you bring to your scrapbook pages. If you're still unsure about what style fits you best, you might start out by borrowing page layout ideas from other scrapbookers. As you create more pages on your own, you'll find yourself repeating certain elements, such as a lettering style, a color combination, or a photo framing technique. And before you know it, you'll have a style that's uniquely you!

IDEAS FOR EXPRESSING YOUR STYLE

Elements such as colors, image styles (stickers, rubber stamps, etc.), repeated motifs, and lettering can unify an entire scrapbook when they're used consistently throughout the pages. This adds your own personal "signature" to the pages in your album. But that doesn't mean that all of your pages have to look the same. And sometimes a particular style just might not be appropriate for the photographs on the page. For example, you probably wouldn't want to use Victorian stickers to decorate a page containing camping photos.

Here are some ideas for creating different looks while still maintaining aspects of your personal style:

Colors • Use lighter and darker shades of your favorite color scheme to suit the photos. Also, select your favorite color background paper in different patterns, such as dots, checks, and plaids—each pattern reflects your color style, but conveys a different feeling.

Images • Look for different artists or companies that create the style of stickers, rubber stamps, or clip-art images you prefer so you can have a varied selection of images to fit your photos.

Repeated Motifs • If you like to repeat an element on your pages, such as a heart or pine tree, look for the image in a variety of forms and styles—stickers, punches, rubber stamps, clip-art, and so on.

Lettering • You can use your signature lettering style for most of the journaling on the page (if it's suitable), but still select a lettering style for the page title that reflects the theme. You can also add variety to handwritten letters by using different colors, serifs, and fill-in patterns.

Remember, you're not limited to using one specific style throughout your entire album, but don't mix styles on the same page. You can apply almost any style to any scrapbook page. Try the unexpected as you develop and express your creative personality.

A Victorian style. By Cheryl Tarrant, Palmdale, California. Paper: Creative Card Company; Scissors: Fiskars (Deckle); Pens: Marvy Le Plume II; Punch: Family Treasures (heart).

• • • • • • • • • • • Designing Spreads • • • • • • • • • • •

AMONG THE MANY decisions to make as you begin designing a scrapbook page is whether you'll use a single-page layout or a two-page spread for each group of related photos. In a single-page design, the photos are arranged together on one page in the album, and facing pages have self-contained designs. A two-page spread involves arranging the pictures on facing pages in the binder so that, when the binder is open flat, the design is visible across left-hand and right-hand pages. Of

course, you can include a mixture of single pages and two-page spreads throughout your album. There are several factors that can help you determine which design style would work best for a particular set of photographs.

THINGS TO CONSIDER

Sometimes a single page is just perfect for the photos at hand, while at other times a two-page spread might be more effective. Here are a few things to keep in mind:

Number of Photos • Depending on the size of your album pages and the amount of cropping you do, you can usually fit two to five photos on a single page. If you have more photos that you want to display together, a spread is one way to arrange them without too much crowding. Spreads also allow you to keep photos in a larger size and still have ample room for page accents and journaling. However, just because you have more photos from an event than will fit on a single page doesn't mean you need to create a spread. Instead, you can create single pages with mini themes, using different-colored background paper and appropriate decorations. Or, you can create a sequence of related single pages to suggest continuity.

Binder Type • Before creating a spread, consider how it will look in the type of binder you're using. Some binders accommodate the spread style better than others do. For example, expandable-spine albums generally lie

flat, with facing pages that are flush, making it easy to create a continuous spread. On the other hand, the rings in a three-ring binder separate facing pages and can be disruptive in a spread design, although spreads can still be created in this type of binder.

Page Theme and Accents • A spread gives you more room to explore a single theme, which is especially nice if you have several page accents (stickers, die cuts, memorabilia, and the like) or want to create a large page title. However, when you have only a handful of photos and page accents, you can often get a more unified look by sticking to a single page. Keep in mind that you can also create individual pages that are similar in theme but not as unified as a two-page spread.

Amount of Journaling • Plan ahead so you'll have sufficient space for the amount of journaling detail that you want to add to your photographs. If you have several photos and a long story to accompany them, using a spread might be a better option. If you're just planning to add short captions, a single page might offer plenty of room.

Personal Style • Finally, take into account your own personal taste. Many photos look just as good whether they're presented on a single page or on a spread, so the decision often comes down to which style you prefer. Some people like the look and flow of two-page spreads in their albums, while others like to keep each page as a separate unit.

Page Sequences

TRY USING SOME of the ideas below if you want to create continuity over a series of pages:

- Use the same general theme and style on each page, including color combinations and lettering techniques.

- Repeat a specific element in the same place on each related page, such as a sticker in the lower corner or a colored bar used as part of the page background.

- Use a similar decorating style on each page, but vary the specific elements. For example, you might fill the empty spaces with tiny stars on one page and with small dots on another page.

- Consider placing a design element on the far right edge of the page, such as a triangular piece of cardstock or a die cut facing outward. This can suggest that the page is continued, and you might even include the words "Continued . . ." or "There's more."

IDEAS FOR DESIGNING A SPREAD

The most effective two-page spreads are those with a strong, unified look. Here are some ways to help improve your spreads:

- Create a border around the entire outside edge of the spread. This is an instant visual cue that the two facing pages belong together.

- Have your page title span both pages. This works especially well if the title is in large, bold letters and is more than one word. However, try not to have too much space between the words or letters so you don't lose continuity, which is often a concern in a three-ring binder.

- Carry an element across the two pages, such as grass or a large die cut (cut the die cut in half so the album will close). You can also create a pop-up that spans the two pages (see page 85 for more information).

- Balance the spread by including corresponding elements in opposite corners (such as the top left corner of the left-hand page and the bottom right corner of the right-hand page) or in all four corners. Or, use mirrored images along each side of the spread.

- Use background paper of the same color for each side of the spread. In addition, repeat the same style of page accents on each page.

- Place your largest photograph on one side of the spread, and then bal-

By Stacy Julian, Salt Lake City, Utah. Scissors: Fiskars (Deckle); Die Cuts: Ellison (crab and sand dollar); Other: letters are tracings from cookie cutters.

ance out the facing page with smaller photos.

Once you've gotten over the initial hump of deciding which layout style to use, the process of creating individual pages and two-page spreads is actually quite similar. Take advantage of all the fun tools and techniques available that can enhance your page and your photographs.

• • • • • • • Design with Color Photos • • • • • •

CREATING A SCRAPBOOK offers so many possibilities for using color—from the background paper to the page accents to the pens and markers—that it's easy to overlook the colors in the photographs themselves. But by paying more attention to the colors in the photos, you can design scrapbook pages that emphasize your pictures without overpowering them.

For starters, make sure you have the sharpest, brightest pictures possible by using quality color film and having your photos developed at a good photo lab. Experiment with different brands of film and have your film developed at several locations to find the combination you like best. As a test, take the same negative to different photo labs and have a print made. Then, compare the results—you might be surprised at the differences in color when you lay the photos side by side.

IDEAS FOR USING THE COLOR IN YOUR PHOTOS

The colors in your photographs can guide you in selecting appropriate colors for other elements on the page, such as the background paper, photo mats, lettering, and page accents (die cuts, stickers, and so on). You can emphasize different aspects of your photographs simply by the color combinations you choose.

Here are a few helpful ideas:

- Look at the main colors in different elements of the photo—clothing, background (sky, grass, sand, water), and so on—and repeat similar colors throughout your page. For example, if the photos are from an overcast beach trip, you might choose more muted colors for the page background elements, such as tan, slate blue, and pale green, rather than bright and sunny colors.

- Select a less dominant element in the photo and then pick up its color for the frame around the photo or other page accents. For example, if a photo has some purple pansies in the foreground, you can mat the photo on purple cardstock to help the pansies stand out.

- Draw attention to your photos by separating them from the page background with double mats of different colors. For example, you might choose a couple of less dominant colors from the photo and use them to create an eye-catching double mat (such as bright red and yellow). Or, you might create a double mat, with the outside mat color being one of the stronger colors from the photo and the inside mat being a bold contrasting color. For even greater contrast, select a patterned paper (such as checked paper) for the inside mat.

- If the background in your photo is pretty much all one color (such as

A muted background can make the most colorful element in a quiet photo stand out. By Sherril Watts, Raleigh, North Carolina. Paper: The Paper Patch; Pens: Zig Super Clean Color; Die Cuts: Ellison; Template: Creative Memories; Corner rounder: Creative Memories.

Sometimes bright colors are the right choice for highlighting the focal point of a photo. By Jenny Jackson, Arlington, Virginia. Paper: Frances Meyer, The Paper Patch; Scissors: Fiskars (Pinking); Die Cuts: Ellison. Photo Corners: Canson-Talens, Inc.

wood paneling or a wide tree trunk), you can help the people stand out more by selecting a page background that's the same color as the photo background. This gives the appearance of a continuous background and works especially well if the photos aren't matted.

- If a color in your photo didn't turn out quite as bright as you would like, try selecting a muted contrasting color for the background and lettering. This can help the photo colors stand out a little more.

- If all the photos on a page are of a similar subject, select a predominant color in an element you want to highlight (such as the clothing of a person) and use that color for the entire page background. Then, select a contrasting color to create single-colored mats for each photo. This helps the photos "pop" off the background.

- If a photo is washed out, pick up the brightest color in the photo and use it for the photo frame as well as other page accents.

- Look over your photographs and decide what kind of feeling you want them to convey—tranquility, excitement, simplicity, and so on. Then,

select colors to help create that mood (and enhance your photos at the same time). For example, vibrant yellow and red are celebration colors, while pastel blue and green suggest a more peaceful setting. Many holidays also have certain colors traditionally associated with them, such as red and green for Christmas.

- Experiment with the order of the colors on double and triple mats.

For example, a darker color on the outside of the frame can make the photo appear larger, while a lighter color on the outside can make the photo appear smaller.

By paying attention to the colors in your photographs, you can enhance the photo subjects and set the right mood for your scrapbook page. But remember that color can also distract attention away from your photos if you're not careful, and that too many colors on the same page can cause your page to look like a confused jumble. Experiment by laying your photos on different colors of paper before you actually cut and glue them, and you'll be able to find the perfect balance.

Color Basics

IN ORDER TO USE COLOR most effectively in your scrapbook, it can be helpful to have an understanding of some basic color principles. Keep the following in mind:

- The color wheel can help you select different color combinations based on the effect you want to create. For example, the three primary colors—red, yellow, and blue—make a striking, vibrant combination. Complementary colors—purple/yellow, blue/orange, and red/green—provide the greatest contrast and can be used to draw attention. Adjacent colors—red, orange, yellow, green, blue, purple, red—blend very well together and create harmony and continuity.

- Colors can convey different feelings and emotions, and artists speak of "warm" and "cool" colors. For example, red is often thought of as an aggressive, passionate color, blue peaceful and soothing, yellow bright and cheerful, and green restful and nature-oriented.

- Neutral colors such as black, white, and gray can be combined with practically any color. Brown can also be used well as an accent with most colors.

• • • • Design with Black-and-White Photos • • • •

CHANCES ARE YOU'VE got at least a few black-and-white photographs stashed away as part of your collection—whether they were taken a hundred years ago or only last month. Black-and-white photos give you a clear and simple composition to work with, and let you focus in on the main subject without being distracted by an abundance of color. Black-and-white portraits can be especially dramatic.

By Valerie Duffy, St. George, Utah. Paper: Paper Adventures (lace); Scissors: Fiskars (Scallop and Seagull); Template: Trace-a-Shape by ESP Corp. (oval).

USING COLOR WITH BLACK-AND-WHITE PHOTOS

One of the first things to consider as you begin planning the layouts for your black-and-white photos is whether you want to use color in your page design. Color can emphasize and complement black-and-white photographs, but it can also compete with them. If you're concerned about color being too distracting, try creating an entirely black-and-white page design. Black-and-white patterned paper is great for adding a little embellishment to your page, and it's available in a wide variety of styles, including dots, checks, and stripes.

If you decide to use color on your page, carefully select shades that will enhance—but not overpower—your pictures. For older, heirloom pictures, stick with softer, muted tones in general, since bright colors can detract from the old-fashioned feel (although warmer colors sometimes work well with black-and-whites). Many times, black-and-white photos look best against dark backgrounds, so you might want to start out testing darker colors such as maroon, plum, navy, and deep green behind your black-and-whites. In addition, try selecting colors such as cream or off-white rather than bright white, which can make some older black-and-white photos look dingy and drab.

For your modern black-and-white photos, bright and bold colors can be a great way to add contrast and a little pizzazz to the page. However, use bright colors sparingly, such as for a die cut or photo frame, and stick with only one or two colors for the best effect.

IDEAS FOR ENHANCING BLACK-AND-WHITE PHOTOS

As you're designing scrapbook pages for black-and-white photos, you have lots of options for bringing out the beauty in the prints. Here are some ideas you can try:

- Mat your photos on cardstock as a fast and easy way to dress them up. For a simple and nostalgic touch, use a double or triple mat of black and white (or cream). Or, experiment with other colors to find a combination that works well for the page theme.

- Create a frame for the photo using cardstock, patterned paper, or stationery. This allows you to focus in on the subject of the photo while still leaving the original print intact. Use an X-Acto knife to cut out the center section of the frame in the shape you want, such as an oval, and then position it over the photo.

By Allison Myer, Mesa, Arizona. Paper: Sunrise Greetings (stationery), The Paper Patch (dots and squares).

- Mount your photos on the page with photo corners. Traditional photo corners, such as black or gold corners, can give both heirloom and modern black-and-white prints an old-fashioned appearance. More decorative photo corners, which can add a touch of style to your page, are also available.

- Use patterned paper for your entire page background. Select a pattern that's not too busy or distracting, and then use coordinating mats or frames for the photos.

- Add an elegant touch with decorative scissors. There are many decorative edges that can complement black-and-white photos perfectly. Try trimming a photo mat or the inside of a photo frame with an appropriate design.

- Include heirloom memorabilia in your scrapbook to help create a stronger link with the people in the photos. Some items can be placed directly on the page, while others might need to be photographed or included in a special case created especially for three-dimensional objects. See page 32 for more information.

- Try hand-tinting your black-and-white photos for a beautiful and striking effect. This technique gives great results on both old and new photos, but should be used only on duplicate prints. See page 100 for more information on hand-tinting.

- Add journaling that details the who, what, when, and where of the photos. This is especially important for heirloom photos and can help your ancestors come alive to future generations. For more ideas on journaling, see page 120.

Designing scrapbook pages to bring out the best in black-and-white photographs might seem challenging at first, but the more pages you create, the more great ways you'll discover to make these special pictures stand out.

Special Considerations for Heirloom Photos

HEIRLOOM BLACK-AND-WHITE photos require special care and handling. Here are a few things to keep in mind as you're placing heirloom photos in a scrapbook:

Cropping • Think twice before cutting any of your older photographs or making any other nonreversible changes, especially if you don't have the negative. Instead, select one of the many ways of framing a photo without altering its original condition. If you want to crop or tint a photo, create a duplicate print first. (If you don't have the negative, you can take the original print to a quality photo lab to have one made.)

Mounting • Be careful not to use a permanent adhesive when mounting your precious photographs in your album, so you can remove them later if you need to. Photo corners are the least permanent mounting option, and photo splits also allow removal.

Quantity • If you have a very large collection of old black-and-white photos, it might not be realistic to attempt to create an elaborate and unique page design for each photo. Instead, you might look for a simple style that will allow you to easily enhance your photos, such as mounting them on similar cardstock mats. Doing this also gives your photos a consistent look. Of course, you can still create special pages for your favorite or one-of-a-kind photographs.

• • • • • Designing Pages for Girls and Boys • • • • •

WHEN IT COMES TO KIDS, people traditionally associate the color pink with girls and the color blue with boys. And while there's certainly nothing wrong with using these color schemes in your scrapbook, using them for *all* of your "girl" and "boy" pages can be a little dull. Fortunately, there are lots of ways you can design fun pages for both girls and boys. All it takes is a spark of imagination and a willingness to try something out of the ordinary.

DESIGN TIPS FOR BOYS' AND GIRLS' PAGES

Creating a scrapbook page that has a specific "boy" or "girl" tone is really quite similar to putting together any

A carefully selected and unusual color scheme can make a very good portrait look its best. By Ellen James, Pleasant Grove, Utah. Paper: Paperbilities; Photo corners: Pebbles in My Pocket.

other page for your album. However, there are several ways you can emphasize the masculinity or femininity of a page without getting stuck in a blue or pink rut. As you start designing your page, keep the following areas in mind, and don't forget to check out page 50 for some general design techniques.

Photo Selection • Boys' and girls' pages don't always have to contain photos of kids doing typical boy or girl activities. Select pictures that capture your child's personality, whether it's your daughter playing with dump trucks in the sandbox or your son snuggling up with his favorite teddy bear. Then use some of the ideas below to give your page design a masculine or feminine touch.

Page Theme • Often, candid shots of kids simply doing everyday kid stuff— like playing outside, getting into mischief, napping, and so on—are used to create traditional boys' or girls' pages. That's because other photos with a more obvious theme—such as a trip to the zoo, a birthday party, or a soccer game—already suggest fairly straightforward choices for colors and page accents, and as a result not as much emphasis is placed on the fact that the child is a boy or girl. When you're designing a boy's or girl's page with

candid shots, you can add some variety by creating a page theme. For example, you might select a common phrase, such as "cute as a button" or "fun in the sun," for your theme. (On the other hand, some people like to steer clear of clichés in their albums.) This in turn makes the design process easier, since you have more definite options for colors, die cuts, stickers, and so on.

Color Scheme • Before you jump right in with pink or blue cardstock for your girl or boy, take a closer look at your photos and try to select colors that match the activity (or disposition) of the person in your photos, as well as your page theme. For example, active or happy events often call for bright and bold colors, while quieter, more subdued times suggest softer, muted colors. Or, you might decide that the traditional pink or blue is just right for the particular page you're working on—and why not!

Page Accents • The style and color of the page accents you select can contribute to the overall boyishness or girlishness of a page. In addition, other elements such as decorative-scissor edges, template shapes, and fonts can affect the tone. Use some of the suggestions below to select those accents that will best enhance your page.

IDEAS FOR CREATING BOYS' PAGES

Boys' pages don't have to be loaded with blue to have an appropriate mood. Try some of these ideas to add excitement to them:

Blue is a perfect background for someone with blonde hair! By Angela Ash, Lewiston, Texas. Paper: DMD Industries (blue denim); Provo Craft (checked); Scissors: Fiskars (Deckle); Fonts: D.J. Twirl, Inspirations, D.J. Inkers; Laminate: Therm O Web.

Even bold elements can enhance the sweetness of the little face in a picture. By Jillyn Wells, St. George, Utah. Paper: The Paper Patch, Memory Press; Pens: Zig; Scissors: Fiskars (Scallop); Stickers: Frances Meyer.

- Select a variety of bright colors, especially for action photos. The primary colors (red, yellow, and blue) are great for creating eye-catching pages. Die cuts are also a fun way to add a splash of color to the page and help enhance your theme at the same time.

- For a slightly different approach, try using darker shades, such as navy, burgundy, and pine green.

- For texture, use patterned paper decorated with plaids and stripes. Dark-colored checked and gingham patterns can also work well.

- Select decorative scissors that have a sharp and definite edge, such as a zigzag or notched design.

- Embellish your page with geometric shapes, such as triangles, squares, and stars.

- Look for stickers, die cuts, fonts, and other page accents that reflect the interests of the boys in your photos.

IDEAS FOR CREATING GIRLS' PAGES

Creating a page that's just perfect for a girl isn't difficult at all. Try some of these ideas to add a feminine touch to your scrapbook pages:

- Don't be afraid to add some spunk with colors such as hot pink (which goes great with black accents) or bright blues and yellows. For action photos of girls, select bright and vibrant colors.

- Select decorative scissors with a rounded design, such as a scalloped or lacy edge.

- Enhance your page with patterned paper consisting of dots or a checked pattern in any color, or try

other specialty papers, such as those with hearts, bows, flowers, and the like.

- Add a quilted look to your page by drawing "stitches" around your photos. In addition, try adding dots or tiny hearts to your lettering.

- Use templates or die cuts to add hearts, flowers, or other shapes that reflect the interests of the girls in the photos (in coordinating colors, of course).

When you want to create a scrapbook page that highlights the uniqueness and joy of your little one, don't limit yourself to the typical colors and layouts. Stretch your imagination and you'll soon discover lots of new ways to emphasize the child's personality while still preserving that little boy—or girl—charm.

• • • • • • • • • • • • Designing Covers • • • • • • • • • • • • •

THE FIRST THING people notice about your scrapbook is usually the cover. The most memorable scrapbook covers are those that catch your eye, identify the contents, and reflect the overall album theme—all at the same time. Designing a cover to do these three things takes a little thought and planning, especially since you're

ring binders provide a pocket on the spine for a small label. Other binders, such as some fabric-covered albums, allow you to sew or glue embellishments fairly easily on the cover but make it difficult to add written text. And still other binders, such as spiral-bound and canvas-covered albums, are perfect for drawing, painting, and

mation they provide. Even if you customize your binder cover, you still might want to create a separate title page to provide additional information or simply reinforce the theme. If your scrapbook is divided into sections, you can also create a separate title page for each section within your album. All of the suggestions below for creating covers apply to title pages as well.

COVER-DESIGN GUIDELINES

A cover or title page serves an important purpose in conveying the contents and theme of the pages that follow it. Designing a cover is similar to designing a regular scrapbook page, but there are some helpful guidelines to keep in mind:

Select a Focus • Decide what—or who—is the main focus of your scrapbook, and then design your cover around something that represents that focus. For example, if you're creating a chronological family album, your cover focal point might be a family portrait. Or, if you're creating a theme album for your summer vacation, you might choose a map or photo of your travel destination. On some covers, the focal point might be simply a one- or two-word title.

Reflect Your Style • Your scrapbook cover should reflect the overall design style of the pages inside. For example, use the same color scheme

working with a relatively small space. But by following a few guidelines, you can create a unique cover that sums up your scrapbook in your own personal style!

COVERS VS. TITLE PAGES

Many binders, such as padded vinyl binders, aren't designed for you to write (or glue or sew) directly on the outside cover, although some three-

stamping right on the surface. (For more information on creating personalized binder covers, see page 48.)

If you can't customize the outside cover of your binder—or if you don't want to—you can create a title page instead that appears as the first page of your album. Title pages are usually quite similar to binder covers in their design and layout as well as the infor-

and lettering style for the cover that you've used for the majority of the pages. This provides continuity and highlights your personality at the same time. If you've used several different styles throughout your album, go with your favorite for the cover! If you haven't created your album pages yet, you might want to wait to create the cover until your album is at least partially full, so you'll have a better feel for which style will be most prominent. (See page 54 for information on scrapbook styles.)

Keep It Simple • You don't want your cover or title page to be overloaded with photos, text, page accents, and other elements. Keep the design simple so your scrapbook's contents can be conveyed in a quick glance. Stick with large, bold letters and only one or two photos.

WHAT TO INCLUDE ON YOUR COVER

There are several elements you can include as part of your cover design to help identify the album contents and show a little of your personality. Remember that you don't want your cover to appear cluttered or confusing, so you don't have to include every suggested item. Here are a few ideas:

Title • Many scrapbook covers have a short title that helps identify the contents, such as "Summer Vacation '94," "The Nelson Family Album," or "My Senior Year." Titles can be especially fun and creative for theme albums. If

you're creating several consecutive albums, you might want to give your scrapbooks volume numbers, such as "Amy's Scrapbook, Volume 1." Or, you can include dates to help keep the albums in order.

Date • Another helpful cover element is the date. You might simply have the year in large numerals, such as 1997. (This can make a stunning cover in and of itself.) Or, if you're creating a chronological album, you might include the months covered, such as April 1996–February 1998. (If you haven't finished the album yet, leave a blank spot to fill the ending date in later.) The date can also be included as part of the scrapbook title, such as "1995 Allen Family Reunion."

Names • It can be fun to weave individual names into the design of your cover. For example, you can position the names of family members around the cover of your family album, or list all the cities you visited on the cover of your vacation scrapbook.

Photos • Photographs are a great way to introduce the main "characters" of your scrapbook. If you're creating a title page, you can mount the photo as you would on any other scrapbook page. If you're creating a cover, you might want to create a separate frame on it that you can easily slide your photo into, using materials such as fabric or cardboard. (This also allows you to change the picture periodically.)

Poems or Quotations • If you have a favorite poem or quotation that relates to the contents of your album, try using it in your cover design. You can make the poem the focal point of the page or repeat it around the edge as a border.

Embellishments • Other embellishments and memorabilia can make a nice addition to your cover, including ribbon, lace, buttons, and so on. (For more embellishment ideas, see page 49.)

LABELING THE SPINE

Finally, don't forget to label the spine, if it's possible on the type of binder you're using. Some binders have a plastic pocket on the spine for holding a cardstock label, and other binders allow you to decorate the spine directly. An identifying label on the spine is particularly helpful when you have several binders stored together on a shelf. Include the name or a brief description of your scrapbook on the spine label, as well as the date, if applicable. Coordinate the label with the colors and style used for your cover. For example, you can repeat an accent from your cover, such as a sticker or shape, on the spine label.

In addition to making it easier to identify the contents, a scrapbook cover or title page can set the tone for your entire album and tie everything together. By taking the time to put a little planning and personality into your cover, you can create a scrapbook that people will find hard to resist picking up.

6

Tools and Techniques

• • • • • • • • • • • • Paper • • • • • • • • • • • • •

PAPER IS INSEPARABLE from scrapbooking. It serves many useful purposes—from providing the main substance of each page to adding color and embellishment to the photographs. You can find paper in hundreds of different colors, designs, and textures. Make your scrapbook pages stand out with bright and bold colors or give them a more classic look with darker shades. Combining and coordinating different paper patterns and colors is a fun and easy way to create eye-catching page layouts.

TYPES OF PAPER

Paper comes in a variety of different types, weights, and styles. The two most common types of paper used in scrapbooks are cardstock and patterned (or decorative background) paper, both of which are available in 8.5" x 11" and 12" x 12" sizes. Cardstock is a stiff, heavier paper (usually 65–80 lb.) that comes in a wide variety of solid colors and can also be found in some textures, such as marble or parchment. (You can also find other heavyweight papers that aren't stiff like cardstock but have unique textures and look great in a scrapbook.)

Patterned paper is generally lightweight and is available in literally hundreds of colors and designs. Patterned paper can be categorized in five different types: backdrops, borders, geometric designs, patterns, and textures. Backdrops have large designs that create a full-page scene, such as a forest or barn. Borders create a frame around the page, leaving the center space free for pictures. Geometric designs include stripes, plaids, and dots, while patterns repeat a tiny motif (such as a heart) or a larger design across the entire page. Finally, textures are imitations of surfaces such as wood, grass, or denim.

No matter which style of paper you choose for your scrapbook, make sure the paper is acid-free so it won't harm your photographs. If you're not sure whether a specific paper contains acid, you can check it with a pH testing pen (see page 33). In addition, you might want to look for paper that is lignin-free and buffered, which can also help prevent deterioration. (For more information, see "Basic Conservation Principles" on page 26.)

IDEAS FOR USING PAPER

There are lots of different ways you can use both cardstock and patterned paper in your scrapbook. Here are a few ideas for utilizing full sheets, as well as leftover pieces and scraps:

Page Backgrounds • Because it's so sturdy, cardstock is generally used as a base for an entire scrapbook page, especially for albums that use sheet protectors and a three-ring binder. If you want to use patterned paper for your page background, it's a good idea to mount it on a sheet of cardstock first to further support and protect your pictures. (You can add a fun contrast by trimming the patterned paper slightly so the edge of the cardstock shows.)

Photo Mats and Frames • You can make the photos on your scrapbook page stand out more by mounting them on one or more layers of colored cardstock or patterned paper. This creates a mat or frame that complements and accents the picture. With so many papers to choose from, the possibilities are endless! (See

Kelli Collins, Mesa, Arizona. Kelli drew food shapes on colorful cardstock, then tore them out to decorate this scrapbook page.

By Ann Smith, Mesa, Arizona. Designer papers: The Paper Patch; Pen: Zig Posterman; Ivy, bird, flower, and bee stickers: Mrs. Grossman's.

"Photo Mounting and Framing Options" on page 94 for more ideas.)

Die Cuts and Punches • Your scraps of paper are perfect for die cuts and punches. Die-cut shapes and letters are commonly cut out of cardstock, but you can also use patterned paper for a distinctive look. And it's easy to add embellishments to your pages by punching out shapes with craft punches; this is a good way to use up your smallest paper scraps. (For more ideas on using die cuts and punches, see page 74.)

Pop-ups and Other Designs • There are many ways paper can add fun and unique designs to your pages. For example, you can make your pages three-dimensional by creating pop-up designs from cardstock. (See page 84 for more information.) Or, create your own custom frames and shapes by carefully tearing the paper.

PAPER TIPS AND TRICKS

There are so many possibilities for enhancing your scrapbook with the beautiful paper available today! Here are just a few tips and ideas you might want to try:

• Make your own background paper from a piece of solid cardstock by stamping an image repeatedly across the page, using a decorative-edged ruler to create a border, or stenciling with a sponge brayer and stamp ink.

• Silhouette part of the background design to create a dimensional effect. This works especially well if a photo would otherwise overlap a portion of the design in the paper. Use a sharp utility knife and then tuck the photo underneath the paper.

• Cut out small designs and motifs from patterned paper to use as embellishments around your page, similar to using stickers or die cuts. You can cut the designs from a separate sheet of paper (either the same style or a coordinating design) or from an area of the paper that a photo is covering up (a neat way to stretch your supplies).

• Experiment with decorative scissors when using patterned paper to see what different effects you can create. (For more scissors ideas, see page 70.)

• If you have a 12″ x 12″ album and 8.5″ x 11″ patterned paper, you can tilt the patterned paper diagonally, leaving opposite corners of the larger page exposed. For 8.5″ x 11″ border papers, you can cut out the middle of the paper, and then make two cuts—one on the top border and one on the bottom. Spread the border out and use coordinating die cuts to cover the empty spaces.

• Keep your paper organized by storing it in acid-free hanging or file folders. For example, you might have one folder for each solid color (such as all shades of blue), a folder for plaids, one for dots, one for seasonal patterns, and so on.

With so many styles and colors of paper available, you're sure never to tire of it! You'll be amazed at the difference a little piece of paper can make.

• • • • • • • • • • • • • • • • • Stickers • • • • • • • • • • • • • • • •

CUTE, ELEGANT, whimsical, or bold—stickers are here to stay! Stickers have long been used in the craft industry to decorate such things as stationery, greeting cards, and invitations. Because stickers are so easy to use and are available in so many styles and sizes, they make a perfect addition to your scrapbook. Stickers can add a subtle touch to a page or create the entire page's theme. You're practically guaranteed to find a sticker to fit any photo or occasion!

STICKER SAFETY

Stickers come in an amazing variety of sizes, colors, and textures. There are full-page stickers, "micro" stickers, border stickers, alphabet stickers, opalescent stickers, metallic stickers,

By Ginny DeRusha, Mesa, Arizona. Pens: Zig Clean Color; Stickers: Mrs. Grossman's.

and the list goes on. With so many different types of stickers—and companies that manufacture stickers—many people have wondered about the safety of using stickers in their scrapbooks.

Most major sticker manufacturers today produce stickers that are virtually acid-free. (Almost all sticker adhesives contain a trace of acid, but in general the levels are low enough that the stickers are considered acid-free.) Typically, the most damage caused by stickers comes from the adhesive. If the adhesive comes in contact with elements such as PVC (polyvinyl chloride), high heat and humidity, or direct sunlight, it will usually either become soft and gooey or become brittle and lose its ability to stick. High heat, humidity, and bright light can also damage the paper used in stickers and cause the ink to fade.

By purchasing acid-free stickers from well-known manufacturers and protecting your album from the damaging elements mentioned above (which can also harm your photographs), you can safely enjoy using stickers in your scrapbook. However, think twice before placing stickers directly on older or one-of-a-kind photographs because you might not be able to remove them at a later date.

IDEAS FOR USING STICKERS

Stickers are one of the most versatile scrapbooking tools because they can be used in so many different ways. And with hundreds of sticker styles to choose from, the same technique can result in

completely distinctive looks. Here are a few neat things you can do with stickers:

Page and Photo Accents • Stickers are perfect for enhancing your page's theme and filling in empty gaps. Position the stickers as accents in blank spaces around your photos—or even directly on some photos. (Make sure the photo is one you won't want to remove later.) Try not to load your page up with *too* many stickers, though, which can give it a cluttered look.

Borders and Frames • Another great way to use stickers is to create page borders and photo frames. Borders look nice whether they're around the entire page edge, along just the top and bottom, or only on one side. You can use stickers to create a frame around your pictures by placing similar stickers all around the photo, or simply positioning one or two in a corner. (There are even photo corner stickers made especially to add some color to the corners.) An easy way to create borders and frames is to combine "line" stickers with a few other stickers that relate to the page's theme. Line stickers—long, thin strips in a solid color or pattern—are designed especially for making borders.

Headings and Captions • To dress up your page, create headings and captions with alphabet stickers. You can also use larger alphabet stickers as ornamental initial caps (for the first letter of a single word or of each word in a phrase) and then write the remainder of the word with a marker or pen.

By Shauna Jackson, Redding, California. Paper: Mara Mi; Pen: Zig Writer; Stickers: The Gifted Line; Scissors: Fiskars (Majestic).

Artwork • Many stickers are designed to interact with each other, allowing you to create custom scenes on your page. By overlapping and positioning stickers, you can become an instant artist! In addition, try some of the ideas below to really add pizzazz to your sticker art.

STICKER TIPS AND TRICKS

Stickers are so simple to use that it's easy to get into the habit of just "peeling and sticking." Here are some tips to help you get even more mileage out of your stickers:

- After placing stickers on a page, embellish them a little with a marker or pen. For example, you can draw in balloon strings, bug trails, movement lines, and so on. Or, outline a sticker with a dotted line to emphasize it.

- When you're designing a page, leave the stickers on their backing as you move them around and experiment with different layouts. If the stickers are on a large sheet, cut around the stickers to separate them (but don't remove them yet from the backing paper). Then, place stickers down lightly at first so you can reposition them if you need to.

- Overlap stickers to create your own custom look. For example, you can place small stickers in the hands of the image on another sticker. If necessary, use a utility knife to cut small slits in a sticker, so you can position another behind it. You can also use the corner of a sticker's backing paper to lift up a sticker slightly as you place others underneath it.

- Don't be afraid to cut stickers or trim them at the edge of a page. For example, you can cut a sticker in half vertically and then place each piece along opposite edges of the page. Or, if a tree sticker is too tall, cut part of the bottom off. To keep stickers from adhering to your scissors, cut them while they're still on the backing paper.

- Try adding dimension to your pages by lifting some stickers slightly off the paper surface. This technique works especially well when you're creating a scene with several stickers. To do this, remove the sticker from the backing and layer three or four pieces of a double-sided adhesive, such as photo splits, on the back of the sticker. (Use more if you want the sticker raised higher off the page.) You can also use foam "pop-up" dots instead of photo splits on the back of the sticker. Then, before removing the backing from the top layer of the adhesive or pop-up dot, sprinkle the back of the sticker with powder, such as baby powder or cornstarch, to remove the stickiness. Shake off the excess powder, remove the adhesive or pop-up dot backing paper, and position your sticker!

- You can create your very own stickers by purchasing a special laminating machine that adds an acid-free adhesive to the back of practically anything, such as clip-art pictures, die cuts, fabric, and so on.

- Keep your stickers organized so you can quickly find what you need and avoid purchasing duplicates. You can store them in a three-ring binder using sheet protectors that have different-sized pockets (make sure you always store your binder upright!), or in a special sticker organizer case that prevents items from falling out.

With so many terrific possibilities, you'll always want to have lots of stickers on hand. Remember that if you can't find stickers you like at one store, shop around a little—you'll find different styles of stickers in craft stores, toy stores, and gift shops. The wide variety of sticker styles available is sure to suit everyone's taste.

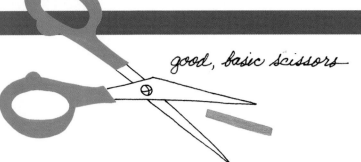

good, basic scissors

• • • • • • • • • • • • • • • • • Scissors • • • • • • • • • • • • • • • •

By Stacy Julian, Salt Lake City, Utah. Scissors: Fiskars (Provincial, inside; Colonial, outside; Scallop, pearls).

ONE OF THE telltale signs of a scrapbooker is a colorful pile of scraps and snips on the floor. That's because scrapbookers spend a good part of their time cutting—from trimming photos to adding decorative edges

decorative-edge scissors

around cardstock mats. Fortunately, there are lots of tools and techniques that can make your cutting chores quick and easy. And you'll be amazed at the varied effects you can achieve with only a pair or two of scissors.

CUTTING TOOLS

A standard pair of straight scissors is a must-have for any scrapbooker, but there are lots of other tools you can use for snipping, cropping, and edging. Some serve a unique purpose, while others have multiple functions. Here's a brief look at the various types of cutting tools:

Straight Scissors • Regular straight scissors are used for tasks such as trimming and cutting out template shapes. Find a good, sharp pair that's comfortable for you to use—several different handle shapes and styles are available. In addition, you might want to keep a pair of fine-tip scissors on hand (such as those used for embroidery), which are great for making small, precise cuts.

Decorative Scissors • Decorative scissors—also called edgers—come in a wide variety of styles, such as scallop, wave, and Victorian. You can use these scissors to add fun designs around the edges of your photos and frames or to give other shapes and letters a textured appearance. You might be surprised at the number of different looks a single pair of decorative scissors can create! See the tips below for some ideas.

Corner Edger • Corner edgers are similar to decorative scissors in that

they have a design built into their blade. However, these tools are designed for trimming only the corners of photos or photo frames. Depending on how you position the paper and edger before cutting, you can get one of four different designs from the same pair of edgers.

Utility Knife • A small, sharp utility knife, such as an X-Acto, is great for making straight cuts—especially since it can be difficult to cut straight with scissors. There are also swivel knives available that are terrific for cutting circles and silhouetting photos. For best results, use the knife with a metal or acrylic ruler and a cutting mat.

X-Acto knife

Paper Trimmer • If you do a lot of cropping, a paper trimmer can be indispensable in providing quick, straight cuts. Paper trimmers come in a variety of sizes and styles—from small, personal trimmers with sliding blades to large, heavy-duty models with cutting arms. You can also find trimmers with decorative blades that help keep your design in a straight line. (Some models have interchangeable design blades.)

Rotary Cutter • A rotary cutter is a hand-held tool with interchangeable blades that cuts as you roll it along paper, cloth, and other materials. Simply attach the design blade you want, and then use a clear acrylic ruler and a cutting mat to make your cut.

By Mary Asay, Mesa, Arizona. Pen: Zig Posterman (Mountain Brown metallic); Scissors: Fiskars (Peaks); Fonts: D.J. Desert, Fontastic!, D.J. Inkers.

Circle Cutter • The fastest way to cut circles out of photos or cardstock is with a device called simply a circle cutter. This handy tool can quickly cut circles in different sizes, usually up to about 7″ in diameter.

DECORATIVE SCISSORS TIPS AND TRICKS

Decorative scissors are a favorite cutting tool among scrapbookers because of the wide variety of available designs and the different results they can achieve. Here are a few tips and techniques to get the most out of your decorative scissors:

• To help you cut straight, pencil in a light line on the back and align the blade of the scissors with the line. (You might also find it helpful to watch the tip of the scissors and keep it on the line.)

• Don't cut all the way to the end of the scissors. Instead, cut partway and then reposition the paper, matching it up with the pattern on the scissors so you get a continuous design. The more you practice, the easier it will be to cut continuous intricate designs!

• If your scissors are grabbing and tearing the paper rather than cutting it, you can try sharpening them up a bit by cutting several times through wax paper or aluminum foil.

• You can create several different looks with the same pair of scissors by experimenting with multiple cuts and cutting in opposite directions. For example, create a strip by cutting along one edge, then cutting

again parallel to the first cut, either matching up the design or offsetting it a little. Or, after cutting the first strip, turn the paper over and cut again for yet another effect.

• Use decorative scissors to cut around the edges of your photos or mats. If you're creating a double mat, try using either the same design or a different design for each mat layer. You can also simply trim the corners of your photo or mat using the decorative scissors—but test the effect first on a piece of scrap paper. (For more information on photo mats and frames, see "Photo Mounting and Framing Options" on page 94.)

• If you're cutting a photo or mat with scissors that make a large design, it can be tricky to make sure both corners along one edge end up at the same point in the design. One way to help solve this problem is first to create a template by cutting a long edge from a piece of cardstock with the

paper trimmer

scissors you're using. Then, lay the template alongside the photo and slide it up or down until the design matches at both corners on that edge. (The best matching position is halfway through a curve, which gives your corners a rounded appearance.) Mark the template where the corner should occur, align the corner of the photo or mat with your template mark, and then match the design with your scissors to start cutting.

• After cutting a mat with decorative scissors, you can accentuate it with a pen or marker. For example, you can draw a solid or dotted line around the inside or outside of the cut.

• Cut out letters and other shapes—large and small—with decorative scissors to add some texture and life to your scrapbook pages. For example, you can make mountain ridges, toothbrush bristles, strands of rope, confetti, and so on. Use your imagination and look for elements in your photos that you can complement with a scissors design.

A pair of scissors is a simple tool, but its usefulness in scrapbooking is immense. From straight snips to edges trimmed with flair, scissors and other cutting tools get the job done with ease!

• • • • • • • • • • • • • • • Adhesives • • • • • • • • • • • • • •

NOW IT'S TIME TO GET down to the sticky stuff. Adhesives serve an essential function in your scrapbook by holding photos, die cuts, and other elements in place on each page. With a wide assortment of adhesives available, choosing one is often a simple matter of personal preference. However, you also need to be careful to select an adhesive that won't harm your photographs or important documents. Learning about the different types of adhesives can help you make the best decision and avoid getting "stuck" with scrapbook pages that fall apart.

TYPES OF ADHESIVES

Adhesives come in many different forms—from liquid to paste to tape. Some adhesives are fairly permanent, while others allow you to later reposition or remove the items you stick down. Some glues and adhesives contain chemicals that are harmful to photographs and can lead to deterioration. But there is also a growing number of adhesives that are acid-free and photo-safe. Here are a few types of adhesives that you might consider using in your scrapbook. (For a list of harmful adhesives, see the "Adhesives to Avoid" sidebar.)

Photo Splits • These small, double-sided adhesive tabs are a favorite among scrapbookers. To use them, all you need to do is place a sticky tab on each corner of the item you want to adhere, then remove the remaining backing paper from each split and mount the item on the page. Photo splits hold items securely in place, but they can also be removed if necessary.

Glue Sticks • Glue sticks are small, cylindrical dispensers of a paste-type glue that you rub on the back of items you want to attach. Glue sticks use either clear glue or colored glue that dries clear, allowing you to tell easily where it's been applied. Over time, however, the adhesive from many glue sticks has a tendency to dry and become brittle, causing items to fall off the page.

Liquid Glue Pens • Glue pens provide an easy way to apply liquid glue—just uncap the pen and "draw" on the area you want to stick down. The pens come with different-sized tips, and, like glue sticks, some glue-pen adhesives change color as they dry. If you attach the item while the glue is wet (before the color changes), the bond is fairly permanent. On the other hand, if you let the glue dry before sticking the item down, you create a temporary bond and can easily reposition the item (although it might not stay down very well).

Photo Corners • Photo corners don't actually stick to the photo you're attaching. Instead, you apply them directly to the scrapbook page (one for each corner), allowing you to slip the photo in and out easily. You can find photo corners in a variety of colors, including transparent, black, and gold. Some photo corners are self-adhesive, while others need to be moistened to activate the adhesive. The easiest way to get photo corners in the correct position is to slip them on the photo first, then activate the adhesive and attach the corners to the page while the photo is still inserted.

Photo Tape • Photo tape—also called a tape runner—is a double-sided adhesive that's similar to photo splits, except it's not divided into tabs or squares. Instead, the tape is on a roll, like regular tape, so you can tear off as much as you need. The adhesive used on photo tape also tends to be more permanent than photo splits and, as a result, items are harder to reposition.

Bottled Liquid Glue • Some types of bottled liquid glue are safe to use with photos. Make sure the brand you select is acid-free, photo-safe, and nontoxic. Liquid glue is generally a little messier than other adhesives and can take longer to dry. Also, some liquid glue can cause your paper to ripple so you might want to test it first on a piece of scratch paper.

Glue Cartridges • A slightly less messy way to apply liquid glue is with a glue dispenser cartridge. These refillable dispensers release a thin film of glue as you roll them along a surface.

Machine-Applied Adhesive • New machines are available (for a price) that apply an acid-free adhesive backing to just about any type of paper, turning it

photo corners

into an instant sticker. (Many of these machines can also laminate.) The adhesive is quite permanent and shouldn't be applied to anything you might want to remove later.

CHOOSING THE BEST ADHESIVE

With so many different adhesives to choose from, how do you know which one is best? The answer generally boils down to the type of material you're adhering and your own preference. In fact, many scrapbookers keep several types of adhesives on hand so they can use the one most appropriate for the particular item they're attaching to a page. For example, you might use photo splits to attach your photographs and a liquid glue pen for die cuts. Here are some guidelines that might help:

Photographs • When you're mounting photographs on a scrapbook page, you probably don't want to use an adhesive that's extremely permanent. It's better to use an adhesive that allows you to remove the photos later, such as photo splits or photo corners. If you're not sure how permanent a particular adhesive is, test it on a duplicate or throwaway photo.

Die Cuts and Punched Shapes • You don't have to be as picky about the adhesive you use for die cuts or punched shapes. If the shape has a lot of small edges, using a glue stick or liquid glue pen makes it easy to cover the entire surface. Larger shapes can often be attached with photo splits or photo tape (which also lets you reposition them). For small punches, many scrapbookers

By Barbara Gardner, Scottsdale, Arizona. Photo corners: Boston International.

like to apply photo tape or photo splits to the strip of paper or cardstock *before* punching. Then, you can punch through the entire thickness (this might take a little more muscle), remove the backing from the adhesive, and you've got yourself a small sticker!

Frames, Mats, and Stationery • Larger paper items such as mats and stationery can also be adhered to a scrapbook page using any of several different methods. Some people like to use photo splits, while others run photo tape or liquid glue along the entire edge. It's all up to you!

Experiment with the different types of adhesives to find the methods that work best for you and your materials. Don't hesitate to use two or three different adhesives on the same page, since some adhesives are simply better suited to particular materials. Before you know it, you'll be "stuck" on the great things adhesives can do!

Adhesives to Avoid

SOME ADHESIVES CAN damage your photographs and other documents. Remember, just because a material is acid-free, it's not necessarily safe for your photographs—it might contain other chemicals and solvents that can be harmful. Here are some adhesives to avoid:

Rubber Cement • The combination of chemicals in traditional rubber cement can cause your photographs to become brittle and deteriorate. Some new rubber cements are safe.

Pressure-Sensitive Tape • Certain types of tape, such as cellophane tape and masking tape, contain acids and other elements that are harmful to scrapbooks.

Spray Adhesive • Spray adhesive is usually flammable—not to mention the mess it can create and the harmful fumes—and should be avoided for scrapbook use.

Other Adhesives with Odors • When an adhesive has an odor and emits fumes, that's usually a sign that it contains elements that can damage photographs.

• • • • • • • • • • Die Cuts and Punches • • • • • • • • • •

COULD YOU USE a surefire method for adding color and pizzazz to your scrapbook pages? Look no further than die cuts and punches. They can instantly transform your scraps of paper into practically any shape imaginable—from hearts and stars to castles and sailboats. With so many choices available, you're bound to find a shape that's just perfect for the page you're currently working on. And because you can use

By Lisa Bearnson, Orem, Utah. Paper: The Paper Patch; Stickers: Provo Craft; Punches: Family Treasures.

paper in any color or pattern, complementing the photos and other elements on the page is a snap!

DIE CUTS

A die cut is a shape that's been cut out with a die-cutting machine. To create a die cut, you place the paper or other material you want to cut beneath the die, which is a steel blade that's been bent into a particular shape, protected in rubber, and mounted on a wood block. Then, you insert the die and paper into the die-cutting machine and apply pressure by lowering a handle or turning a crank (depending on the type of machine). The result is an instant, perfect shape, created faster than scissors ever worked!

Die cuts range from tiny shapes about 1″ high to shapes that fill an entire page. In addition to object shapes such as balloons, cars, and dinosaurs, you can find die-cut shapes for letters, borders, and photo frames. The shapes are often quite intricate, with areas cut out from the middle and scored detail lines. Die cuts can be created from several different materials, such as cardstock, patterned paper, and fabric.

Most people don't own their own die-cutting machine because of the cost of both the machine and the individual dies. However, many scrapbook stores and educational supply centers have die-cutting machines (and a wide variety of dies) available for customers to use. In addition, you can purchase precut shapes from many scrapbook and craft stores.

IDEAS FOR USING DIE CUTS

Try some of these great ways to use die cuts in your scrapbook:

Accent Your Page • Choose a shape that corresponds to the photos or theme of your page, then simply position the die cut in an empty space or overlap it with a photo. You can also combine die-cut shapes to create your own unique artwork.

Create Headings • Use the letter and number die cuts to add bold headings instantly to your pages—no penmanship required!

Frame Photos • Die cuts can make great frames for your photos. Just trim your photo to fit inside the shape, or, if the die cut has an opening, position it over the photo.

Add Details • Emphasize your die cuts a little by outlining them with a pen or marker. You can also draw in details such as eyes, add movement marks, or even write captions directly on die cuts.

Combine Different Colors • Just because a shape is originally cut out of a single color doesn't mean you have to leave it that way. Many die cuts

large punch

have pieces that are meant to be cut out of a contrasting color, such as the berries with a holly leaf or the rind portion of a watermelon. In addition, die cuts that start out as single units can be divided into different colored sections, such as the stem on a group of cherries or the segments of a beach ball. To create a multicolored die cut, first make cuts of the entire shape in every color you want to use. If the die cut is in a single piece, cut each section apart. Then, combine the colored pieces to create a stunning result!

Create Shadows • Add a neat effect to your die cuts by creating a "shadow." To do this, simply cut two of the same shape out of contrasting colors. Position one color behind but slightly to one side of the other on the page to give it a shadowed look. This works great with letters as well as other shapes.

PUNCHES

Punches might be considered mini die-cutting machines, since you can quickly punch out a variety of shapes in different sizes. Punched shapes are generally much smaller than most die cuts, and, like sticker motifs, they can be used to embellish a scrapbook page. Punches offer one of the best ways to use up all your paper scraps!

The most common type of punch used by scrapbookers is a "craft punch," which rests on a hard surface (such as a table) and has a button on top that is pressed to create the shape. Craft punches come in several different sizes—from mini punches with shapes only an eighth of an inch tall to large punches with inch-high shapes. There are punches that come with more than one design in the same punch, silhouette punches that create a reverse image in a frame, and punches designed specifically for corners. You can also find hand-held punches that create a variety of tiny shapes.

IDEAS FOR USING PUNCHES

Here are a few suggestions to help you get the most out of your punches:

Make Silhouettes • Use your punches to not only create individual shapes that you can glue to your pages, but to also create "silhouettes," where a coordinating color of paper is placed behind the area that was punched so it shows through. This method works great for corner punches and also for creating a unique border across a page or photo frame.

Use the Punched Pieces • Some punches, such as a circle punch, are very versatile. Experiment by cutting punched shapes in half or by punching in several places on the paper, then combining the pieces to create a new shape. (A circle punch is one of the best punches for a new scrapbooker to acquire.)

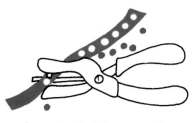

hand-held punch

PUNCHING TIPS AND TRICKS

- Try turning your punch upside down so the button rests on the table. This allows you to apply pressure more easily when punching (especially with jumbo punches), and also helps you see exactly where the punch will be aligned on the paper.

- If you're punching several shapes in a row for a silhouette border, you can get even spacing by using a ruler to mark dots on the back where you want the center of each shape, and then placing the punch upside down so you can position the center dot correctly. Or, you can align the previous punch in the paper strip with a specific spot on the edge of the punch itself each time you move the strip down.

- If your punch is sticking or tearing the paper, try punching through wax paper, aluminum foil, or even fine-grained sandpaper.

- As you acquire punches, it's helpful to create a reference sheet of the shapes at your disposal: punch out a shape with each of your punches and glue the shapes to a sheet of paper.

Die cuts and punches are a fun and easy way to spruce up your scrapbook pages. The toughest part is deciding which shape to try next!

•••••••••••••••Templates••••••••••••••••

HAVE YOU EVER cut an oval freehand and then kept trimming it because it was always just a little lopsided? Or drawn a heart that didn't turn out *quite* right? Templates are simple tools that can help you easily and accurately accomplish several big tasks— from cropping photos to creating shapes to adding instant letters and borders. Templates—also called stencils—guide your pen or pencil perfectly as you trace the outline of a shape or letter, which you can then cut out or color in. It's a great, quick way to draw when your own hand might not be as reliable as you'd like it to be.

TYPES OF TEMPLATES

A template usually consists of a thin sheet of stiff plastic with different shapes cut out of it, such as circles, stars, and flowers. Some templates have basic shapes that are designed specifically for cropping photos, such as circles and ovals in a variety of sizes, while others have more intricate shapes that work better as embellishments on the page to enhance its theme. Templates can also come in the form of rulers with decorative edges.

There are two basic ways you can use a template. First, you can trace the

A template can be used to make a cutout or an outline to color in

outline on a photograph or piece of paper and cut out the result, which can then be mounted on your scrapbook page. Second, you can trace the shape directly on your scrapbook page and then color it in if you want. Alternatively, you can use a sponge and stamping ink to stencil the template image directly on the scrapbook page instead of tracing it with a marker.

If you don't want to purchase templates, you can create your own fairly easily. Start with a piece of moderately sturdy cardboard, such as poster board or a file folder. Then, trace or draw the shapes you want, leaving about 0.5″ around each shape and around the edge of the page for a border. Cookie cutters make great shapes, as do many simple die cuts. To get several sizes of the same shape, use a photocopier to

reduce and enlarge it. After tracing, use an X-Acto knife to carefully cut out each shape. The remaining sheet will be full of holes, but it will make a great custom template!

IDEAS FOR USING TEMPLATES

Templates can be used to enhance practically any element of a scrapbook page. Here are just a few ways:

Crop Photos • You can focus in on the subject of your photographs by using a template to cut away unnecessary background details. Photos are commonly cropped into standard shapes, such as circles and ovals, and they can also be cut into many other fun shapes, such as flowers or stars. To crop a photo, lay the template over the photo until you see the portion you want. Experiment with different shapes and sizes before actually cutting to find the one that works best for that particular picture. Then, use a wax pencil to trace around the template outline. Cut the photo with a pair of straight scissors and wipe off any remaining residue from the pencil with a clean, soft cloth.

After cropping a photo with straight scissors, you can mount it on a colored mat, as explained below. For more information about deciding which photos you should crop, see "How (and When) to Crop or Cut" on page 98.

Design Photo Mats and Frames • It's easy to create photo frames and mats with the help of templates. For example, after cropping a photo into an oval, you can cut a slightly larger oval out of cardstock or patterned paper and use it as a mat behind the photo. (If you don't have the template shape in a larger size, you can mount the cropped photo on cardstock and trim an even distance around the edges, matching the shape.)

In addition, your frame doesn't have to be the same shape as your photo. Try using a template to cut a shape out of cardstock and then overlap a smaller rectangular or oval photo on it. Or, cut a template shape out of the center of a rectangular piece of cardstock and place the outer part over the photo as a frame. (This avoids actually cutting the photo.) As with photos, you can trim the frame or mat with decorative scissors for an added flair. (See "Photo Mounting and Framing Options" on page 94 for more frame ideas.)

Add Lettering • There are many alphabet templates and stencils available

that can help you add bold headings to your pages in a flash. You'll find letter styles to suit practically any theme. You can either trace the lettering right on your page or cut the letters out of coordinating paper.

Create Page Accents • Like die cuts, templates provide shapes that you can position around your page to fill up empty space and help enhance the page's theme. Simply trace the template on cardstock, cut it out, and attach it to the page. For a more colorful result, trace and cut the same template out of several different colors, then cut the shapes into sections and combine select pieces into one shape. You can also trace or stamp the shape directly on the scrapbook page and color in any details.

Add Borders • Rulers and templates with decorative edges are a great way to add page borders quickly. Trace the border directly on the page and then embellish it if you want with stickers and other drawn lines. Or, you can trace the border along one edge of a strip of cardstock, cut it out (this works best for larger designs), and attach it along an edge of your scrapbook page.

STORING YOUR TEMPLATES

If you have a lot of templates, storing them can be a little tricky.

By Linda Cottrell, Johnston, Iowa. Paper: The Paper Patch; Pens: Zig Clean Color; Scissors: Family Treasures (Deckle); Punch: Marvy Uchida (Star); Templates: Creative Memories.

Because they have so many edges and corners, templates have a tendency to get caught on each other, creating a big, tangled mess. To keep your templates organized, you can store them in individual file folders. Or, you can store them in a three-ring binder by punching holes along the edge (many templates are already three-hole-punched). Insert a sheet of cardstock (also three-hole-punched) between each template in the binder to keep them separated. If you have quite a few templates, you can organize them further in the binder with tabbed dividers that separate the templates into categories, such as geometric shapes, holidays, and so on.

The next time you need to crop a photo or add a page border, pick up a template and put it to work. Cutting out ovals and hearts was never so easy!

POCKETS ARE GREAT for storing all those little, miscellaneous items that you don't quite know what else to do with—things like pennies, tickets, and buttons. In addition, pockets help protect smaller objects from getting lost or damaged. Scrapbook pockets—or "pocket pages"—are easy to create and provide a fun way to include more than just photographs in your album. For example, you can use a pocket page to hold items and memorabilia that you don't want to attach permanently to a page, such as certificates, invitations, hospital bracelets, pressed flowers, and the like. (For more ideas on the types of mementos you can save, see "Memorabilia" on page 22.)

TYPES OF POCKET PAGES

You can create pocket pages in any type of album; an album with an expandable spine or a three-ring binder is ideal. Pocket pages are of three different types:

Full Pocket • A full pocket page consists of two regular scrapbook pages glued together along the left, right, and bottom edges, leaving the top open. The front page is usually cut down slightly to allow easier access to the pocket, and die cuts or other designs can be used to define the top edge. In addition, the front of the pocket can be decorated as a regular scrapbook page with photographs and other items.

Half Pocket • A half pocket page is similar to a full pocket page, except that only a half sheet is glued on top. As a result, the pocket is not as deep, but it will still hold most items securely. The pocket generally takes up the entire width of the page and can be trimmed along the top edge with decorative scissors. Both the front of the pocket and the top portion of the back page can contain decorations or journaling.

Shaped Pocket • You can create pockets of any shape or size by simply gluing a cutout shape to the main scrapbook page along three edges, leaving the top open for inserting items. The shape might be a die cut or a custom shape that you've cut out from cardstock. For example, you can create a large, full-size pocket that's in the shape of a balloon or cupcake. Or, you can create small, rectangular pockets on a page, with each pocket holding an individual item, such as a hospital bracelet or lock of hair.

HOW TO MAKE A FULL POCKET PAGE

Full pocket pages work best in albums where the pages can be removed, such as three-ring binders and expandable-spine albums. You can also create full pocket pages in spiral-bound albums, even though the pages can't be removed. To create a full pocket page, follow these steps:

1. Start with two regular scrapbook pages, such as two sheets of cardstock or two pages from your album (remove them if necessary). The pages can be the same color or of different colors.

2. Decide how you want to design the top edge of the pocket. At least

By Bonnie Pace, Dallas, Texas. Gingham Paper: The Paper Patch.

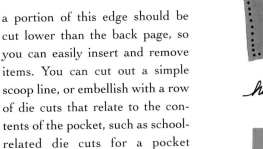

half pocket

a portion of this edge should be cut lower than the back page, so you can easily insert and remove items. You can cut out a simple scoop line, or embellish with a row of die cuts that relate to the contents of the pocket, such as school-related die cuts for a pocket containing report cards and artwork. Be creative!

If you're using die cuts, position them an inch or so from the top of the page and attach them to the page with your favorite adhesive. (If the die cuts are overlapping, remember to position the lower ones first.) Otherwise, pencil in the line that you want to cut, such as a curved or zigzag line. If your page is from an expandable-spine album, make sure that you won't cut off the top staple (or other fastener) that holds the page in the album.

3. Use a pair of straight scissors to trim along the top outline of the die-cut shapes or to cut along the line you just drew.

4. Now you're ready to join the two pages together. Turn the front page over and apply an adhesive along the left, right, and bottom edges. Photo tape (also called a tape runner) works well for this, since you can lay down a continuous strip of adhesive. Turn the page back over, line up the edges with the second page (using the bottom edge as a guide), and stick them together!

5. Finish by decorating the front of the pocket as you would any other scrapbook page and inserting your mementos in the pocket.

HOW TO MAKE A HALF POCKET PAGE

Half pocket pages are very similar to full pocket pages. To create a half pocket page:

1. Remove one page from your album or select a piece of cardstock for the main scrapbook page (the back of the pocket).

2. Then, choose a piece of cardstock for the pocket itself. This can be any color, but it should be the same width as your page. Cut the pocket piece down to just under one-half of the page height.

3. If you want, trim the top edge of the pocket with decorative scissors, or add die cuts along the top edge as explained above in the full pocket section.

4. Attach the pocket to the back page along the left, right, and bottom edges, using glue or photo tape. (See the full pocket section for more information.)

5. Finish the page by adding any decorations you want to the front of the pocket and the top portion of the back page.

HOW TO MAKE A SHAPED POCKET PAGE

Shaped pocket pages can be created easily in any type of album, since you don't need to remove the pages.

1. Cut the pocket shape you want out of a piece of cardstock or select a die cut. Make sure the shape is large enough to allow adhesive along three edges and still hold the items you want to place in it.

2. Turn the shape over and apply adhesive along the left, right, and bottom edges. If the shape has a lot of curves and corners, you might find that a glue stick or liquid glue adhesive works better than photo splits or photo tape.

3. Simply attach the shape where you want it on the page.

4. Add any decorations, slip in the pocket items, and you're done!

Pockets have always been a great place to store and protect those important little things—and scrapbook pockets are no exception. Instead of keeping your mementos stored away in a drawer, include them in scrapbook pocket pages so they can be enjoyed again and again.

• • • • • • • • • • Computer Software • • • • • • • • • •

By Christine Moffat, Deerfield, Illinois.
Scissors: Fiskars (Ripple); Punch: McGill
(Foot); Software: Creative Photo Albums,
Dog Byte Development.

COMPUTERS HAVE done wonders to make all sorts of tasks faster and easier—including creating scrapbooks! There are dozens of great software products on the market that are designed specifically to help you put together a scrapbook. Whether you need a border, page headings, artwork, or an entire layout idea, your computer can help—without requiring you to be the least bit artistic. Scrapbooking software is generally quite easy to use, especially if you're already familiar with getting around on a computer. (If you're a little intimidated by computers, have someone show you the basics—you might be surprised at how easy it is!)

Note: Many scrapbookers have wondered about the safety of using printer ink in their albums. Because scrapbooking is a fairly new hobby, there hasn't been a lot of extensive research done yet in this area. Initial tests show that the ink used in ink-jet printers is acid-free but not permanent, since it smears if it gets wet. If you're concerned about using printer ink, back your photos with acid-free cardstock and position them so they don't come in direct contact with any ink on the page.

WHAT YOU NEED
Before you run out and buy a software program, take a minute to become familiar with the equipment you already have. That way, you'll be able to select programs that will work well on your system. Here are some helpful things to know before choosing software:

Computer Setup • Be aware of your computer's operating environment, such as Windows 95, Macintosh, Windows 3.1, or DOS. Many programs have separate versions for different environments (such as Windows and Macintosh), or they only work on specific systems (such as Windows 95 and not Windows 3.1). Check the package to make sure it will run on your computer. In addition, know whether your computer has a CD-ROM drive—if not, you'll need to find programs that are available on 3.5" floppy disk.

Printer Type • Software programs generally work with most types of printers, including laser and ink-jet printers. If you have a color printer, you might want to look for a package with precolored images. If not, you can still print color images (they'll print in shades of gray), but you might focus instead on finding software with black-and-white images that you can add color to yourself.

Programs Already Installed • In order to use many clip-art programs, you need to have a program already installed on your computer that can import the clip-art images, such as a word processing, page layout, or drawing program. Check the manuals of the programs you have installed to see what graphics formats they support. (And you might even find that these programs already have clip-art images that you can use in your scrapbook.)

Finally, before you purchase any software program, read the package over carefully for any other special requirements.

CLIP ART
Computer clip art can save you lots of time, especially if you like to include drawings in your scrapbook but aren't much of an artist. Clip-art images come in a wide variety of sizes and styles. There are three different ways you can incorporate clip art into your scrapbook:

Print, Cut, and Glue • Import the clip-art image in your word processing or page layout program and make it the size you want. (Many programs also let you manipulate graphics and add neat effects.) Then, print the image on acid-free paper, cut it out, and attach it to your scrapbook page with your favorite adhesive. This

scrapbooking software is easy to use

method allows you to place the image exactly where you want it, and it works especially well if you have album pages that can't be run directly through the printer.

Print on the Page • If your album pages are removable and can fit in your printer (such as cardstock pages used in a three-ring binder), you can print the images directly on the page. Use your word processing or page layout program to position any images and text you want, and you're all set to print. You might want to print a test page on scratch paper first to make sure everything is in the correct place.

Print and Trace • A final option is to print the images on regular paper and then trace them on your scrapbook page with the help of a light box or window. This gives your pages a more handmade feel. After tracing, you can add color to the images if you like. Many people also like to trace images from coloring books and other printed material that they haven't created electronically.

FONTS

Fonts are another favorite computer tool of scrapbookers. There are hundreds of different fonts available for both Windows and Macintosh computers, and you can find them in specific font packages as well as in many clip-art and page layout programs. Fonts help you easily create eye-catching page titles and captions, and are one

option for adding journaling to your page. Just like clip art, you can print the text on acid-free paper, then cut around it and attach it to your page, or you can print it directly on your scrapbook page. Try printing text and titles on paper of a contrasting color, or one that matches other page elements, such as photo mats or die cuts.

BORDERS

Borders help enhance the theme and provide a visual frame for an entire scrapbook page. Many clip-art packages include border graphics, and there are also several software programs that contain nothing but borders. Borders are generally printed directly on a scrapbook page, but they can also be printed on separate paper and then glued to the main page (similar to how you might use decorative paper).

PAGE LAYOUTS

If you're stumped for layout ideas, try using one of the software programs that have predesigned scrapbook pages. These programs are generally geared toward 8.5" x 11" pages and contain all the elements you need for a great page (except the pictures, of course). You can mix and match different borders, clip art, fonts, and so on to create your page background. Some programs have layouts that contain "place markers" indicating where you

might position your photos. Other programs will let you insert pictures that are in an electronic format.

If you find yourself running out of time or ideas for your scrapbook, take a look at the many terrific software programs available for scrapbookers. (One of the side benefits of purchasing a program for your scrapbook pages is that you can use the clip art and fonts with all your other computer projects as well.) Find a program that contains a style of clip art or fonts that you like so you get good use out of it, and pay attention to how other people have used computers in creating scrapbook pages. And most of all, have fun!

By Mindy Thomas, Santa Monica, California. Pen: Sakura Micron Pigma; Scissors: Fiskars (Deckle); Software: Creative Photo Albums, DogByte Development.

WANT TO KNOW a secret for bringing a so-so scrapbook page to life? Add some texture! Of course, one of the best ways to add texture is with memorabilia items that help tell the story of the pictures on the page (see page 22). But there are lots of other ways you can add texture to your pages even if you don't have any special mementos. For example, you can crimp some of your cardstock, weave a ribbon frame, or decorate your page with everyday items such as buttons and fabric.

By Phyllis Wallin, Long Valley, New Jersey. Decorative Papers: Paper Pizazz, Hot Off The Press; Corner edgers: Fiskars.

PAPER CRIMPING

Crimping is a technique that creates a ripple effect on paper, similar to what you'd find on corrugated cardboard. This texture usually is added with a paper crimper—a hand-held tool containing rollers that the paper is squeezed through. Paper crimpers come in different sizes, with the smaller ones limited to paper 3″ wide and the larger ones accommodating paper up to 6.5″ wide. (If you want crimped paper in a full-size 8.5″ x 11″ or 12″ x 12″ sheet, you can purchase special acid-free corrugated paper.)

To use a paper crimper, first trim the paper you want to texture into the desired final size or shape. For example, use a cardstock photo mat, a die cut, or another paper design, such as grass or ocean waves. Draw any designs or lettering on the paper *before* crimping, since it's difficult to write on the paper after it's textured. Then, simply place the paper in the edge of the crimper, grasp the handle, and turn the key to move the paper through.

IDEAS FOR USING A PAPER CRIMPER

Crimp at Different Angles • You can create diagonal designs by running the paper through the crimper at an angle.

Crimp Only Part of the Paper • For example, create a cardstock photo mat about 1″ larger than the picture and then crimp each corner separately—beginning at the point and ending just past the edge of the photo.

Crimp Folded Paper • If you fold a piece of cardstock in half and run it through the crimper at an angle, the crimped lines go in opposite directions when you open the paper back up. This makes a great effect for leaves or even turkey feathers!

Crimp Paper Twice • After crimping a piece of paper once, crimp it a second time at a different angle. You can create a lot of eye-catching diamond and checkerboard effects using this technique.

Crimp Accordion-Folded Paper • One stunning design you can create with a paper crimper is the herringbone look, which works especially well as a photo mat. To do this, begin by folding a piece of lightweight paper accordion-style (paper with a metallic look works especially well). Then, crimp the folded strip at an angle, and open the paper up. Magnificent!

IDEAS FOR WEAVING

Another great way to add texture to your scrapbook pages is with weaving. You can weave ribbon, lace, raffia, and even strips of paper in and around your pages. There are several different weaving techniques that you can use in your scrapbook:

Paper-Strip Weaving • This is one of the easiest forms of weaving and involves simple strips of paper. First, cut strips of cardstock or other paper to weave through your main background page. You can also tear the strips (rather than cut them with scissors) for a more handmade look. Then, use a utility knife to cut straight slits in your background paper where you want to weave the strips through. Make sure they're big enough for the strips to fit through, and try to space them evenly. Weave the strips in and out of the slits and you're finished! If you want to create a basket look, cut several horizontal or vertical strips across a portion of the page (making sure you don't go all the way to the edges), and then weave several strips right next to each other, alternating which section is visible on top.

Punched-Hole Weaving • Here's a technique for weaving a material such as ribbon, lace, or raffia around a page or photo frame. If you're going to be weaving around a shape with straight sides, use a ruler to pencil a light line where you want your punched holes to be. Then, use a small, rectangular punch, such as a quarter-inch punch, to make a series of holes around the shape. After you punch one hole, position the edge of the punch right next to the punched hole to measure even spacing for the next one. Do this all the way around, turning the punch diagonally at corners. Then weave the ribbon, raffia, or other material through the holes.

(The material should be slightly smaller than the size of the punch.) Tie the ends together to finish it off.

Over-the-Top Weaving • For a Western look, you can weave cord, string, or twine over the top edge of a piece of cardstock or other material. Begin by punching holes with a small, round punch around the edge of the area you want to frame. Then, weave the cord through a hole (coming from the back to the front), over the top of the material, and in through the back of the next hole. Continue this all the way around and tie it off when you're finished.

IDEAS FOR ADDING OTHER TEXTURES

When you want to add a little extra texture to a scrapbook page but aren't quite sure what to use, take a

By Audrey Corrine Birch, Rancho Palos Verdes, California. Scissors: Family Treasures (Scallop); Punch: Family Treasures.

look around your house. Many common items can become the finishing touch on your page. Here are a few ideas:

- Use ribbons to add hair bows or balloon strings.
- Glue buttons around the page.
- Add some frill with a lace doily.
- Cut out designs from fabric or wallpaper scraps.
- Create things like cowboy ropes and fishing lines with some twine or string.
- Use thread to add stitches or "tie" the holes in die-cut buttons.

No matter what extra materials you add to your page, do your best to make sure they're acid-free and won't harm your photographs. Use a good adhesive to hold them in place and let your imagination go wild!

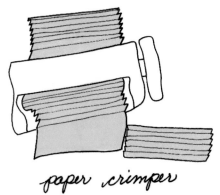

paper crimper

AS A GENERAL RULE, scrapbook pages are basically flat. That stands to reason since you need to be able to close and store your album easily. However, it is possible to add a whole new dimension to your scrapbook—without increasing its overall thickness—by creating what's known as a "pop-up." With just a few folds of cardstock and a little imagination, your photographs will practically jump right off the pages. Pop-ups can also make your scrapbook interactive, encouraging viewers to lift and open various elements.

Pop-ups work best in albums that don't require sheet protectors, such as expandable-spine albums and spiral-bound albums. If you use a three-ring binder for your scrapbook, pop-ups can only be effective if the page is removed first from the sheet protector. Since doing this repeatedly can wear down both the page and the photos, you're probably better off using other techniques to enhance your album, such as including memorabilia (see page 32) or adding textures (see page 82).

HOW TO MAKE A PHOTO POP-UP

A basic pop-up consists of a folded cover that hides a photograph. When the front of the cover is lifted, the photo "pops up" off the page. To create this type of pop-up:

1. Select the photo that you want to use for the pop-up picture inside and trim it as needed. Many people silhouette the pop-up photo to make it more effective. (You can also use a die cut or other shape instead of a photo.)

2. Make the folded cover of the pop-up by simply folding a piece of cardstock in half (the fold goes at the top). Or, you can attach two identical die cuts to each end of a small folded piece of cardstock so they're aligned with each other. When folded, the cover should be about twice the height of the inside photo.

3. Make a tab to attach to the photo so that it pops up when the cover is opened. To do this, cut a strip of cardstock that's wide enough to

support your photo and is the same height as the folded cover.

4. Assemble your pop-up by first folding the tab in half. Then attach the photo to one side of the tab, positioned with the folded edge of the tab toward the center of the photo and at least 0.5" of the tab sticking out from the bottom of the photo. (You can use photo splits, a glue stick, or another adhesive.) After gluing the photo, fold back the lower edge of the top tab so it's even with the bottom of the photo. Turn the photo and tab over, and fold back the other side of the tab to the same position. This creates the sections where the tab will be attached to the cover.

5. Next, open the cover so it's flat, with the inside faceup. Position the photo at the angle you want, aligning the center folds of both the tab and the cover. Glue the small, folded sections at the bottom of the tab to the top and bottom of the cover. Close the cover to crease the folds and make sure that the photo doesn't show from the outside.

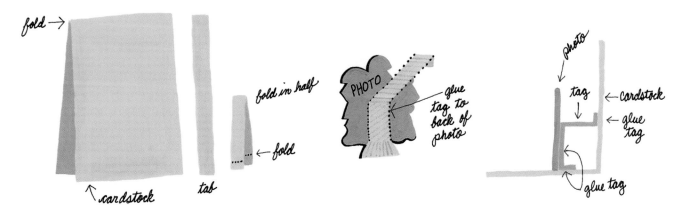

6. Finally, mount the cover on your scrapbook page by applying an adhesive to the back of the cover and positioning it where you want it on the page. Decorate the front of the cover with any stickers, die cuts, captions, or other elements. (If your pop-up doesn't lie quite flat at first, it should flatten over time with the continued pressure of the album pages.)

HOW TO MAKE A POP-UP FOR A TWO-PAGE SPREAD

A second type of pop-up that you can create is one that spans two scrapbook pages. This makes a fun addition to a two-page spread, and works especially well as a banner heading for the two pages. (This type of pop-up doesn't work in three-ring binders because it's connected to facing pages.)

To create a two-page pop-up banner, follow these steps:

1. Cut a strip of cardstock the width and length you want for your banner. If you don't have an individual piece that's long enough (for example, if you want the banner to extend the full width of both pages), cut the longest strip you can for the middle portion. Then, cut two extra strips to add to each end, but don't attach them just yet.

2. Fold the strip in half (the middle portion if you cut more than one piece), and then fold it in half again. Unfold the second fold you just made and *reverse* one of the fold lines so that both ends of the strip point away from the center.

3. Unfold the entire strip and set it down with the center fold pointing up. You might find it easier to decorate the banner with die cuts, markers, or stickers at this point, before attaching it to the page. For a fun look, try positioning die cuts so they slightly overhang the banner edges in the pop-up portion. Also, remember that you'll be able to lengthen the banner a little later if you need to.

4. Apply an adhesive on the back of each end of the strip, up to the first fold lines. Attach the strip to the adjoining scrapbook pages, positioning it over the center so that the middle section pops up slightly. Make sure the center fold of the strip is aligned with the center of the two pages.

5. If you cut extra strips of cardstock to make your banner stretch across the entire width of the spread, glue the strips to each side of the page, making the banner appear continuous.

6. Finally, close your album carefully to make sure that the pop-up section folds correctly. (The center fold should move toward the outer edges of the album.)

Pop-ups can provide a whole new level of fun, creativity, and enjoyment for working on your scrapbook. Experiment with different pop-up shapes and folds and you might be surprised at just how three-dimensional a scrapbook can be.

Photography

• • • • • • • Cameras for Scrapbookers • • • • • • •

A GOOD CAMERA is an essential tool for anyone who wants to record and preserve memories. Your camera determines how easy it is for you to take pictures, and also affects how well the photos turn out. Cameras come in a wide variety of sizes, styles, qualities, and price ranges. By learning about some of the different styles and features available, you can select a camera that's suitable for your skills and lifestyle.

35 mm camera

35MM CAMERAS

The 35mm camera is the most popular type of camera in use today by both amateur and professional photographers. Some 35mm cameras are fully automatic, while others have manual settings to give you control of certain features. There are two basic types of 35mm cameras:

Point-and-Shoot • A "point-and-shoot" camera is also referred to as a lens-shutter camera, since the viewfinder lens is separate from the actual picture-taking lens. Point-and-shoot cameras are usually fully automatic, with autofocus and automatic film

handling (advancing and rewinding). They also come with a wide variety of features, such as zoom lenses, different flash modes, and date/time stamps.

Single-Lens Reflex (SLR) • With an SLR camera, you view the scene through the same lens that takes the picture. SLR cameras often give you manual control of exposure and focus settings, and also allow you to interchange lenses, flashes, and other accessories. Professional photographers typically use these cameras.

In general, SLR cameras give you higher-quality pictures than point-and-shoot cameras. However, amateur photographers usually prefer automatic point-and-shoot cameras for easily capturing daily events (especially the candid and spontaneous ones). And if you're willing to spend a little extra money, you can get a high-caliber, multifeatured automatic camera that produces excellent results.

ADVANCED-PHOTO-SYSTEM CAMERAS

The increasingly popular advanced-photo-system (APS) cameras come in a variety of styles and price ranges, but they all share several unique features:

- A special film cartridge (24mm) that only has to be dropped into the camera. On some cameras, the film can be taken out mid roll and replaced with a different roll (such as a different speed film), then returned again to continue where you left off.
- A choice of three different sizes for each photo, selected by simply set-

ting an option on the camera. APS cameras can take photos in the classic format (the same as 35mm), high-definition television (HDTV) format (slightly larger and suitable for wider shots), or panoramic format (for very wide scenic shots).

- A magnetic coating on the film that records information (using technology similar to a computer disk). This information includes the date, time, and frame number, as well as information about flash usage and lighting, that is automatically communicated to the film-processing equipment. The date and time are printed on the back of each photo.
- Negatives that are stored in the original film canister, keeping them free from dust and fingerprints. In addition, each developed roll includes a "photo index," making the reprint process easy. However, APS film (and processing) is generally more expensive than 35mm film.

advanced-photo-system

DISPOSABLE CAMERAS

A special type of camera that is a favorite among scrapbookers is the dis-

disposable camera

posable—or single-use—camera. You can find both 35mm and APS disposable cameras in a variety of styles, including panoramic and waterproof. While these cameras don't have the features and lens quality of a regular camera, they work well for certain situations. For example, you can take a disposable camera on a river-rafting or hiking trip and not worry about your regular camera being damaged. They are also great if you want to let kids take their own pictures.

CAMERA FEATURES

If you're shopping for a new camera, consider these features:

Autofocus • This feature is indispensable for taking quick snapshots. Also look for the ability to focus on off-center subjects.

Zoom • A zoom lens is perfect for getting close to your subjects without being too intrusive, and it produces sharper images than closeups made with a regular camera. Look for a powerful zoom lens, such as 115mm, which allows you to get really close.

Date Stamp • Having the date and time imprinted on each photo is a great timesaver when later sorting and organizing your pictures. If you don't like

the date on the front of the photo, look for a camera that can print on the back.

Flash Modes/Red-Eye Reduction • Different flash modes—such as auto flash, red-eye reduction, fill flash, and night flash—help make sure your pictures turn out just right.

Timer • A timer allows you to get in the picture yourself once in a while!

Investing in a good camera will make your scrapbook that much better by providing you with clear, sharp prints. Find a camera that meets your needs, and then don't forget to keep it

handy and loaded so you won't miss those once-in-a-lifetime shots.

Other Accessories • In addition to the features on the camera itself, look for other accessories that can help enhance your picture-taking experiences. For example, a good carrying case can protect your camera as well as give you a convenient place for storing your manual and extra film and batteries. A tripod is another useful accessory that can help you take clear photos, especially of scenery and groups of people.

Taking Care of Your Camera and Film

TO GET THE BEST POSSIBLE pictures, you need to take good care of your camera and film. Here are a few tips for keeping everything in tiptop condition:

- Don't leave your film where temperatures may be high, such as in a car on a hot day, since heat can adversely affect the film quality. After buying film, store it in the refrigerator until you're ready to use it.

- Before buying, check the expiration date of the film, which is usually located on the side of the film package.

- Change the batteries in your camera at least once a year to keep everything running at full speed. The battery affects not only the flash but also the shutter movement and automatic film advancement. Keep an extra battery on hand, but out of reach of children.

- Load and unload your camera out of direct sunlight, since bright light can fog the film. If you're outdoors and can't find a shady spot, use your body to help block out the sun while you load or unload the camera.

- Keep your camera lens clean. Gently blow away dirt and wipe it clean with a lint-free cloth.

- Protect your camera from sand or ocean spray by storing it in a plastic bag until you're ready to take a picture. Similarly, make sure your camera is shielded when taking pictures in the rain.

- Store exposed film out of bright light and out of the reach of small children. Take your film in as soon as possible to be developed.

• • • • • • A Short Course in Photography • • • • •

CHANCES ARE YOU'RE taking new photos all the time to capture your newest memories, which are just as important as those long past. One of the best things you can do to make your scrapbook better is to improve the pictures themselves. After all, as the main focus on each page, photographs are the heart and soul of a scrapbook. But don't worry—you don't have to be a professional photographer to take good pictures. Just learn some of the basic tips and techniques given here, and then practice, practice, practice. You're sure to be pleased with the results!

GET TO KNOW YOUR CAMERA

The first step toward taking better pictures is to become familiar with your camera's features and settings. Take a few minutes to read through your camera manual and learn how to use the available options. For example, you might discover that you can manually turn on the flash, focus on an off-center subject, reduce red-eye, or delay picture taking with a timer. In addition, your manual will give you important information, such as the range where your flash is most effective, the type of battery required, and the minimum distance for clear pictures. If you've lost your manual, take your camera to a quality camera shop and ask a specialist to explain the functions or order a new manual for you.

CHOOSE THE RIGHT FILM

An important factor in determining picture quality is the type and caliber of film used. With 35mm film, you have the choice of several different ISO speeds—the most common for amateur photography being 100, 200, and 400. (ISO refers to the International Standardization Organization, which adopted the numerical system for indexing the sensitivity of film.) The higher the speed, the faster the film records the image and, thus, the faster the camera shutter opens and closes the aperture. Fast 400 film is more sensitive to light, so less light is needed. More light is needed by slow 100 speed film. Faster film generally results in brighter pictures and makes your camera's flash more effective. (Faster film is usually more expensive for these reasons.)

Select a film speed that is most appropriate for the pictures you plan to take. High-speed film, such as 400, is good for all environments, but works especially well for action shots and low-light settings. Low-speed film, such as 100, should generally be used only with bright lighting and mainly outdoors. For all-around use, 200 film works well for indoor and outdoor photos, as well as for moderate action shots. After loading the film, make sure your camera is set to the proper ISO speed. Many cameras automatically detect the speed of the currently loaded film.

STAY IN FOCUS

To get the sharpest pictures possible, place your camera on a tripod or other stable surface to keep the camera still. If you can't set the camera down, plant your feet firmly on the ground, keep your elbows in, and hold the camera

stay in focus

with both hands tightly against your face. In addition, remember to squeeze the shutter button *gently* to reduce any camera movement. Many people press the shutter too hard, which causes the camera to shake and results in blurry pictures. Even a slight jiggling of the camera can reduce sharpness, which is especially apparent if an enlargement is made.

WATCH THE LIGHTING

Lighting plays a crucial role in how well a photograph turns out. Make sure your subject is well lighted, but watch out for squinting or harsh shadows. If you're taking photos outdoors, have your subjects face away from the sun to eliminate squinting. Then, use your camera's flash to help lighten any shadows on their faces—a technique called "fill flash." Many cameras allow you to turn on the flash manually to get this result. Flashes also help to freeze action and produce sharper pictures—just be sure you're within your camera's flash range for it to be effective (usually 4–12 feet).

Overcast days are surprisingly some of the best for taking outdoor pictures because the softer lighting eliminates squinting and flatters skin tones. And don't let rain scare you away—rainy days can make colors more vibrant and give almost any subject an extra glisten. Just protect your camera from moisture by using an umbrella or shooting from under a shelter. If you're going to be around lots of water, such as on a river-rafting trip, you might want to use a disposable, waterproof camera.

KEEP THE BACKGROUND SIMPLE

Before you snap a picture, check around in the viewfinder and make sure the background isn't too cluttered

watch the lighting

or distracting. Your goal is to keep the focus on the subject of your picture, so avoid busy backgrounds as much as possible. If the background *is* distracting, try shooting from a different angle, zooming in a little closer, or moving the subject to a new location altogether. In addition, watch out for things like poles or tree branches that might appear to be "growing" out of a person. If you're indoors, be aware of any backlighting that might affect the picture. Sometimes the best background is one that's plain enough to direct all attention to the subject, such as an indoor wall, a wide tree, or a clear, blue sky.

GET A LITTLE CLOSER

One mistake that amateur photographers commonly make is taking pictures

from too far away. Concentrate on the *people* in the picture and don't worry about squeezing in all of the extra surroundings. Going a step further, fill the frame with the most important part of people—their faces. You don't need to see everyone's feet in each picture. Instead, focus on their eyes and capture the expressions on their faces. Your photos will come to life, be more enjoyable to look at, and be less likely to need cropping later!

Try this: the next time you're ready to snap a picture, take one or two steps forward first. If your camera has a zoom lens, don't be afraid to use it. However, be careful not to get *too* close—most cameras have a minimum distance at which they take sharp pictures (usually about 3–4 feet). Also, sometimes using a flash at a close distance can result in too much light and washed-out faces. Check your camera's recommended flash range to avoid this problem.

If you do want to capture some of the breathtaking scenery in your photos, have your subject stand closer to the camera in the corner of the picture, and choose the smallest lens opening to maximize depth of field. Or consider leaving the people out of a few shots. Besides, you'll never recognize those tiny people in the center of the picture anyway!

TAKE PICTURES AT EYE LEVEL

A great way to make eyes the focus of a photo is to take pictures from the same level as your subject. For example, if you're taking a picture of a child sitting on the ground, sit down yourself (or get on your knees). Of course, there's nothing wrong with shooting pictures from other angles for variety, but in general, staying on the same level allows you to fill the frame with the subject of your picture.

TRY A NEW ANGLE

There's no rule that says every picture you take has to be a horizontal shot. Turn the camera vertically once in a while, especially when you have no

take pictures at eye level

more than three people in the picture. This allows you to focus in on your subject without including unnecessary background. Before you snap the shutter, walk around your subject and test out different angles and positions through your viewfinder until you find the one that works best.

Also, you can give your pictures a fun, new look by shooting from unex-

pected angles. For example, take a photo while lying on the ground, or climb up high and shoot straight down. For outdoor photos, avoid positioning the horizon in the middle of the picture, which cuts your pictures in half. Instead, use a low horizon for a feeling of spaciousness (especially with a blue sky), or a high horizon to suggest closeness. (And don't forget to keep the horizon level!)

PLACE THE SUBJECT OFF-CENTER

Does it seem like all of your photos have the subject right in the middle? Centering each subject not only makes your photos less interesting, but it also wastes space on each side of the pho-

The Red-Eye Problem

A COMMON OCCURRENCE in snapshots is a phenomenon known as "red-eye," where the subjects' eyes appear as bright red dots. Red-eye is caused by the light of the flash reflecting off the retina of the eyes. The closer the flash is to the lens in the camera (and the more powerful the flash), the greater the degree of red-eye. Try these tips to reduce red-eye in your photos:

- Increase the amount of light in the room when taking indoor photos with a flash.

- Ask people you are photographing to look just to the right or the left of the camera. If they are wearing glasses, tilt the glasses down or have them turn their heads slightly to avoid having the flash reflect off the glasses.

- If it's available on your camera, use the red-eye reduction mode, which is usually a low-light flash that appears before the regular flash. By having your subjects look at this light, their pupils contract and don't reflect as much of the regular flash.

- Look for a camera that has a greater distance between the flash and the lens, as in cameras with a pop-up flash.

If your photos still end up with some red-eye, you can purchase a red-eye pen to help remove the effect. Red-eye pens are easy to use and work well in restoring the natural eye color. All you need to do is dab the tip of the pen on the photograph until the red color is gone.

tograph. Add some variety by positioning your subjects in other locations. A good guideline to follow is the "rule of thirds": as you frame your picture, mentally divide the viewfinder into thirds both horizontally and vertically creating nine squares. Then, place your subject anywhere but the middle—the four intersecting points are also visually appealing.

Many cameras automatically focus on whatever is in the center of the viewfinder. However, you may be able to override this setting to focus on an off-center subject. Check your camera manual for the specific adjustments you should make, and experiment with different settings.

ADD SOME DEPTH

When you're capturing a scenic view, add some depth to your picture by including objects (or people) in the foreground. Items such as trees, fences, or rocks help add a sense of depth and make the picture more appealing. Trees with overhanging branches make a great natural frame. Check your camera manual—and experiment—to find the settings that result in a sharp, clear picture.

CAPTURE MORE THAN POSES

Instead of having people smile and

try a new angle

pose for the camera in every picture, snap several action and candid shots. Capturing people in action makes them look more natural and relaxed. If your subjects aren't active, prompt them to do something like give a hug or catch a ball. When you're photographing a sporting event with fast action, use a high-speed film, such as 400. Then, press the shutter button a split second before the peak in the action to capture the crowning moment.

Some of your most rewarding pictures will be the candid ones taken when your subjects are unaware of the camera. Candid shots can capture people's true personalities—whether they're smiling, laughing, crying, or not even looking at the camera. For a few guidelines on taking candid pictures, see the sidebar on page 93.

Now that you're armed with some

tips and techniques for taking better pictures, you're ready to start practicing. Take lots of pictures, experiment with your camera, and don't get discouraged if they don't all turn out. Remember, for every handful of mediocre shots, there's usually one great picture. (Think of how many pictures a professional photographer snaps in a single photo session!) The more you practice, the better you'll become at capturing your memories!

add some depth

• • • • • • • How to Take Great Snapshots • • • • • •

CAPTURING MEMORIES on film—from the unexpected moments to the special occasions—is a never-ending process. Events happen every day that are perfect for photographing and recording in a scrapbook. You can take even better pictures for your scrapbook by remembering a few simple photography tips and techniques. Along with the suggestions in "A Short Course in Photography" on page 88, try some of the methods below for great scrapbook snapshots.

By Cheryl Bartels, Apache Junction, Arizona. Green paper: Hot Off The Press; Tan paper: Memories Forever; Pen: Sakura Micron Pigma; Scissors: Fiskars (Peak, Leaf); Template: Fiskars; Bamboo: Cheryl's own design.

BE PREPARED

The most memorable events often come at the most surprising times, so it's important always to have your camera loaded and ready. Life won't usually wait around for you to hunt down your camera. Keep your camera loaded with film, and also try to have an extra battery and roll of film on hand. Take your camera with you as you head out the door so you won't miss great photo opportunities. If your camera is too large to carry with you easily, why not consider packing a disposable camera on special outings?

KEEP SHOOTING

Professional photographers realize that not every picture will turn out to be a masterpiece, so as a result they snap lots of shots. The same holds true for any photographer—the more pictures you take, the better your chances are of getting some really good ones. (And remember you don't have to put *every* photo in your scrapbook.) As an added bonus, taking lots of photos helps you become more familiar with the different features on your camera, and your next pictures will be that much better.

Take a variety of pictures and poses so you have a good mix for your scrapbook pages. Include a few group shots and get lots of closeups of people. Don't forget to snap several action and candid shots as well.

TELL THE STORY

Your photographs can help tell the story on a scrapbook page, especially if you take pictures at the beginning, middle, and end of the event. For example, instead of just taking pictures of fishing during a camping trip, include a few of setting up the tent first, and then cleaning and cooking the fish afterward. Action and candid shots are invaluable in relating the story through photos. (Of course, you can still add journaling later to fill in the details.)

When you're traveling, record some of the personal moments, such as unpacking in your hotel room, getting on the local subway, or getting comfortable on the airplane for the trip home. Don't forget to take pictures of the group around signs that indicate where you've visited, such as the entrance to a national park or the welcome sign at a state border. And, in addition to special occasions and trips, take pictures of the normal, everyday routines (especially children's) at your home to portray a "day in the life."

BE UNIQUE

Add some variety to your scrapbook pages by snapping some out-of-the-ordinary shots. For example, take a roll or two of black-and-white film. Black-and-white pictures add a dramatic look to your scrapbook and can be a refreshing change from bright colors. Also, the absence of color helps focus more attention on the people in the pictures. For a striking effect with black-and-white pictures, try tinting them. (See page 100 for more information.)

Be creative by shooting from new camera angles—like shooting straight down from a high position—or by experimenting with different light sources. Don't be afraid to try a feature on your camera, a new film speed, or a shot you'd never think would turn out. It just might! The unique photos will make great additions to your scrapbook.

FOCUS ON PEOPLE

The best scrapbook photos are those that showcase the individual personalities of people. Fill your pictures with people—especially faces and expressions—to bring your scrapbook pages to life. When you're at a crowded location, such as an amusement park, step off the busy pathway so you can compose your picture without being jostled around (and so you don't end up with strangers in your photo). Single out people in a crowd to add personality and interest to your pages.

INCLUDE YOURSELF

A common syndrome of family photographers is that they're so engrossed taking pictures of others that they forget to be in the pictures themselves

once in a while. Hand the camera over, and let someone else take a shot or two. Let different family members take turns being your photographic helper. Learn how to use the timer and automatic shutter on your camera, if it has one. Even if you don't like to be photographed or the pictures aren't posed exactly the way you'd do it, what's important is that *your* unique personality is recorded as well.

By Deanna Lambson, Sandy, Utah. Green plaid paper: Little Extras; Frog stationery: MM's Design; Scissors: Fiskars (Scallop, Ripple); Leaf die cuts: Ellison; Fonts: Funky, Pebbles Tracers, Pebbles in My Pocket.

Taking the Best Candid Shots

CANDID PHOTOGRAPHS are often the most enjoyable and can really capture the personality of a subject. Here are a few suggestions for getting great photos:

- See what happens. Give your subjects something to do or hold on to, then wait and watch. For example, have them interact with a pet or hand them an object such as a flower or ball.

- Make everyone comfortable. Dress children so they'll feel relaxed and free to interact with their surroundings.

- No smiling for the camera! Look for characteristic facial expressions and natural body language. Place your subjects in a new or interesting environment. For example, take a field trip to a discovery park or farm.

- Keep your distance. The subject will soon lose interest in you (and your camera). Then, use a zoom lens to get a close shot without being distracting.

- Be patient. The most memorable pictures often come at unexpected moments.

• • • • Photo Mounting and Framing Options • • • •

MOUNTING PHOTOS in your scrapbook is one of the most enjoyable aspects of the entire scrapbooking process. Instead of just placing photos in an ordinary album, you can watch them come to life by creating unique photo frames. Frames not only add color and excitement to your scrapbook pages, but—more importantly—they emphasize the photos. And the best part is that you can use all of your fun tools to create frames that are as simple or as elaborate as you want.

The possibilities are endless! Here's an overview of ways to mount photos, plus dozens of great frame ideas.

HOW TO MOUNT PHOTOS

When you're ready to mount your photos on a scrapbook page, just follow these three easy steps:

1. Select the size and shape of the photo. Decide what shape would work best for the photo. For example, do you want to leave the photo in its original size? Do you want to crop it into a shape, or silhouette the people in it?

Or do you simply want to trim the corners with decorative scissors? For help in deciding whether a photo should be cropped, see "How (and When) to Crop or Cut" on page 98.

2. Next, create the frame. Determine what extras—if any—you want to add to the photo. This is where you can let your creative juices flow! For example, you might decide to simply place the photo directly on the scrapbook page and draw a border around it with a pen. Or, you might

By Stacy Julian, Salt Lake City, Utah. Scissors: Fiskars (Ripple); Stickers: Frances Meyer.

use the common technique of mounting the photo on a piece of colored cardstock and then trimming the paper around the photo, creating a mat or frame. You can further enhance a photo frame with things such as stickers and die cuts. The ideas given a little later show just a few of the possibilities.

3. The final step is to lay your photos out on the page and mount them with an adhesive. (Adhesives can also be used in the previous step to mount the photo to the frame.) Which type of adhesive should you use? The best choice often depends on the size and shape of that particular photo. For example, if the photo is a fairly common shape, such as a rectangle or circle, photo splits (small double-sided stickers) are quick and easy. On the other hand, if your photo is silhouetted or cut into a shape with a lot of small edges, a glue stick or liquid glue pen might be better to help hold everything in place.

You should also consider how permanent you want the photo to be in your scrapbook. If you want to be able to remove the picture from your scrapbook in the future, photo corners are probably the best choice. Photo splits are a good semipermanent adhesive that holds photos securely but allows you to remove them if necessary. Other adhesives are more permanent and difficult to remove. For more information on the different types of adhesives, see page 72.

IDEAS FOR FRAMING PHOTOS

Adding creative frames around your pictures is a great way to liven up your scrapbook pages while still keeping the emphasis on the photos themselves (which is, after all, what you want people to look at). Frames can be simple or elaborate, fun or classic—whatever suits your style! Photo frames are also one of the best ways to strengthen the overall theme of the scrapbook page. Select colors that highlight aspects in the pictures themselves, and have fun with coordinating and contrasting shades. Here are just a few ideas to get you started creating frames for your photos:

Single Mats • An easy way to add an eye-catching frame is to back the photo with a piece of colored cardstock or patterned paper. After cutting your photo to the desired shape (if you want to crop), use an adhesive such as photo splits to mount the picture on a piece of acid-free cardstock or paper. (Lay the photo over several different colors to determine which one brings out the best tones in the picture.)

By Sandi Genovese, Irvine, California. Scissors: Fiskars (Scallop); Stickers and border tape: Mrs. Grossman's; ¼" Press-on Letters: C-Thru; Die Cuts: Ellison.

Then, trim the paper to leave a frame—or mat—around the picture and mount the entire unit on the scrapbook page. If you have several pictures on the same page, carry out your theme by using one or two colors to mount all of your photos. For a slightly different look, cut the mat the same size as the photo and then offset the two to create a shadow effect.

Multiple Mats • In addition to creating a mat with a single color, you can enhance your photos even more by mounting them on two or more pieces

By Becky Higgins, Peoria, Arizona. Background paper: Provo Craft; Flower stickers: Frances Meyer; Pens: Zig Writers, EK Success; Scissors: Fiskars (Stamp).

By Martha Vogt, Mesa, Arizona. Scissors: Fiskars (Seagull, Wave); Stickers: Mrs. Grossman's; lace effect: pen markings.

of coordinating cardstock. Try contrasting colors, alternating patterned paper with solids, or making each mat layer a different thickness.

Textured Mats • Spruce up your mats even more by using decorative scissors or corner edgers. The combinations are endless—you can trim the photo with the scissors and place it on a straight-cut mat, cut only the mat with the decorative scissors, or cut both decoratively. You can also cut just the corners of the photo (and mat, if you want), using scissors or a corner edger. Experiment with different edges on each mat layer for a unique result. (For more ideas on using decorative scissors, see page 70.)

Photo Corners • Acid-free photo corners come in a variety of colors, such as black, gold, and even clear. Photo corners are a cinch to use and allow you to remove the photo later if you need to. Simply place the corners

on the edges of the photo (the photo should be square or rectangular), and then adhere the corners to the page. You might find it easier to moisten or remove the backing from one corner at a time to get them positioned correctly. In addition to standard photo corners that hold the photo in place, photo corner *stickers* are available in a variety of colors and styles. These stickers can be placed over the corners of a photo to add vibrancy or just an old-fashioned look. (Adhere the photo to the page first with photo splits or a glue stick.)

Text • Another easy and unique photo frame is plain and simple text! After mounting your photo on the scrapbook page or a cardstock mat, write words around the border of the picture. You might repeat the names of the people in the photo or give a brief caption or description. This type of frame serves a dual purpose because it also provides important

information about the photograph.

Hand-Drawn Borders • Pick up a pen and draw your own frame around a photo. You can draw dashed lines, stars, dots, or any repeating pattern. Alternate pen colors for a lively effect. You can also use pens to accent photos that have a cardstock mat. If the mat or photo was trimmed with decorative scissors, try drawing a pattern such as dashes or dots along the edge in a contrasting color.

Paper Frames • Paper frames designed specifically for scrapbook photos are available in dozens of styles and colors. Or, you can create your own frames by cutting out designs from stationery and patterned paper. In addition, many clipart programs have frames you can print, color, and cut out.

Die Cuts • Die cuts are often positioned on a scrapbook page to enhance the overall theme, but they can also be used to help frame photos. For exam-

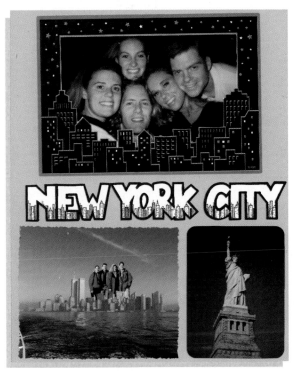

By Becky Higgins, Peoria, Arizona. Paper: FMI; Scissors: Fiskars (Deckle).

By Barbara Silvester, Portland, Oregon. Bandanna paper: Provo Craft; Polka-dot paper: The Paper Patch; Computer clip art: Giddyup Thangs (boot); Photo corners: Canson.

ple, you can position die cuts around the edges or corners of a matted photo, use larger die cuts that have an opening as the entire photo frame, or create custom backgrounds for silhouetted photos. For more ideas on using die cuts, see page 74.

Punches • Paper punches serve a dual purpose when framing photos. First, you can punch out small shapes to place around the edges or corners of the photo. And second, if you're using a multilayered mat, you can punch out of the top mat layer, allowing the contrasting color below to show through. This technique works especially well with punches created specifically for corners. (See page 74 for more information on punches.)

Rubber Stamps • Some rubber stamps are specifically made to serve as frames—just stamp the design on the page (or mat) and trim the photo to fit in the frame area. Other rubber stamps can simply be repeated around a photo

or used in the corners of a mat. (The section beginning on page 112 has a lot of other ideas for using rubber stamps.)

Stickers • Similar to die cuts and punches, coordinating stickers can be used to accent or create a photo frame. Large stickers work well in the corner of a frame to help emphasize a certain aspect of the photo, and small stickers can be placed along the edges of the photo or mat.

Custom Designs • With a little bit of creativity, you can create your very own unique photo frames. Cut designs for your frame out of cardstock or patterned paper, or even try tearing it for a striking effect. Draw, stamp, or stick on items to further enhance it. Overlap photos, tilt contrasting background mats—you can end up with some striking results!

FRAMING TIPS AND TRICKS

With so many different ways to frame your photos, it's easy to add personality and pizzazz to your scrapbook. To

best display your creativity:

• Stick with one general theme or style for the photos on the same page so it isn't too cluttered or overwhelming.

• Help your larger and more attractive photos stand out by using more elaborate or bold frames with them. Use simpler frames for smaller photos, and remember that not every photo on the page needs to have a frame.

• If mounting your photos on mats or ready-made frames, do this *before* mounting any part of the unit to the scrapbook page.

• Remember to leave room on the page to add journaling and other information that describes what's happening in the photos. (See pages 120–129 for more ideas.)

• Don't spend *too* much time worrying whether certain colors really match or if you're cropping a photo to the right shape. Go with your instinct and have fun!

• • • • • How (and When) to Crop or Cut • • • • •

IT DOESN'T TAKE LONG for a new scrapbooker to become familiar with the term "crop." Cropping refers to cutting photos into different shapes and sizes (although sometimes the term crop is used to indicate scrapbooking in general). Ideally, we'd frame a perfectly balanced photograph in the viewfinder of our cameras, but this is rarely possible (especially when taking shots spontaneously)—even for professional photographers!

Cropping has many benefits: it lets you fit several photos on a single page, remove unattractive or unnecessary elements from a picture, and direct focus to the main subject. However, cropping is *not* for every photo. So how do you know when to reach for your scissors or knife? Use the guidelines below to help you first determine which pictures to crop, and then choose the cropping technique that will work best for that photo.

DECIDING TO CROP

Some photos are better left in their original shape, while others can be enhanced with cropping. Deciding which photos to cut should be done with care, since the alterations you make aren't always reversible. Keep in mind these guidelines:

- Never crop your best photos, especially those that your children or grandchildren might want to frame someday. In addition, many candid shots that capture our day-to-day lives are more meaningful when they're left intact.

- Don't cut "instant" photographs, such as Polaroid prints. Cutting these photos can release chemicals that might damage other items in your scrapbook.

- Think twice before cropping out items that help place a photo in the context of your life. Many details, such as cars, homes, and clothing, might have historical or sentimental value in the future.

- Check to see if you have duplicates or similar photos. For example, if you have several shots of the same event, choose the best one (or two) to keep intact as the main focus, and then feel free to crop the others to enhance the page. And remember always to keep your negatives, since you never know when you might want an extra copy of a photo you've cropped.

CROPPING TOOLS AND TECHNIQUES

Once you've decided which photos to crop, the next step is to determine how you want to crop them. Cropping can be as simple as trimming the edges and rounding the corners, or as detailed as cutting the photo into a unique shape or silhouette. Here are a few ideas:

Trim the Edges or Corners • A fast and easy way to crop a photo is to trim the edges, keeping the photo in a square or rectangular shape. Use a paper cutter or an X-Acto knife and metal ruler to cut a straight line. (It's hard to cut straight with scissors.)

Remove any unwanted "dead" space around the margins of the image—you don't have to trim the same amount off each side. For example, you can cut the top and bottom off an outdoor photo to create a narrow rectangle and give the impression of a wide-angle lens. For a softer look, try rounding the corners slightly with a corner rounder. You can also clip just the corners of a photo using decorative scissors or a corner edger.

Use a Template • Templates can help you quickly crop your photos into a variety of different shapes—from ovals to stars to Christmas trees. The shapes add to the overall page theme while at the same time narrowing the focus to the subject of the picture. Templates are also a great way to fit several photos on the same page, because of the smaller size of the cropped pictures. To use a template, position it over the photo and trace around the edge with a blue wax pencil. Use regular straight scissors to cut out the traced shape, and clean up any remaining residue from the wax pencil with a soft cloth. For more ideas and information about templates, see page 76.

Cut Circles • Circles and ovals are two of the most common shapes used when cropping pictures, because they're eye-pleasing and not too distracting. One of the easiest ways to crop into a circle is to use a circle cutter. This handy tool quickly cuts photos or cardstock into perfect circles the size you specify (generally up to about 7″ in diameter).

By Stacy Julian, Salt Lake City, Utah. Birdcage paper: Pet Paper Pizazz, Hot Off The Press/Fiskars; Scissors: Fiskars (Dragonback); Paper Crimper: Fiskars; Birdcage stencil: Stacy's own design; Font: *The ABCs of Creative Lettering* by Lindsay Ostrom.

If you don't have a circle cutter, you can crop photos into circles or ovals by using a template.

Create Your Own Shape • If you can't find a template with the shape you need, or if you want to use your photos in a page design based on unusual shapes, try creating it yourself. Draw the shape first on cardstock or other paper and then trace it onto your photo.

Enhance with Silhouettes • Silhouettes are a fun way to call attention to a scrapbook page, and they make great page accents. A silhouette is created by cutting around the outline of a person or a group of people in a photo—leaving none of the background. The best photos to use for silhouettes are duplicate or other "extra" photos, where the background details aren't that important to keep. Use an X-Acto knife (swivel knives work great) or a pair of scissors to trim carefully around the person in the photo. For best results,

leave a tiny border around the object you're silhouetting. You can mount the silhouette on colored cardstock or simply position it on the page as you might a die cut. A neat effect you can achieve with silhouettes is to place them on top of other, uncropped photos. This makes your photos appear to jump right off the page!

Combine Shapes and Silhouettes • A unique cropping technique that gives your pages depth is to crop most of the picture with a template but then also silhouette a portion of the photo, such as a foot or leg that extends outside the shape of the template.

Add a Frame • If you don't want to cut a photo but do want to hide some distracting details, place a paper frame over the photo. Several ready-made frames are available in a variety of paper and colors, or you can create your own with cardstock.

MOUNTING CROPPED PHOTOS

After cropping a photo, consider how

you want to mount it on the page. You can use practically any of the mounting and framing ideas in the "Photo Mounting and Framing Options" section on page 94 to liven up a cropped photo. One common technique is mounting the photo on a coordinating piece of cardstock that's trimmed to the same shape as the photo.

As you position the photo on the page, try tilting it at an angle for a different look. Or, place the cropped photo slightly over the edge of the scrapbook page, and then trim the edge so it's flush with the page. If you've silhouetted several photos, you can combine and overlap them to make an interesting collage.

Finally, remember when you're taking your pictures in the first place to move in a little closer to your subject. Then, you won't have to crop as much later! But if you *do* need to crop, these tips and ideas can help you get fantastic results.

• • • • • • Tinting Black-and-White Photos • • • • •

BLACK-AND-WHITE photos have a timeless, classic beauty—no matter how recently or long ago they were taken. You can add a unique charm to black-and-white photographs by hand-tinting all or part of them. Hand-tinting a photo isn't as difficult as it might sound, and the results make a stunning addition to any scrapbook. There are two different materials you can use for hand-tinting: photo oils or hand-coloring pens. Each offers its own advantages, as you'll see below.

GETTING STARTED

Before you jump in and start hand-coloring all of your photos, keep these considerations in mind:

By Debbie Hewitt, Agoura, California. Scissors: Fiskars (Bubbles); Stickers: Stickopotamus; Hand-coloring pens: SpotPen.

- Use a duplicate print or enlargement for coloring—never color an original print. If you don't have the negative, you can easily have one made from the original photo at a custom photo lab.
- If you don't have any black-and-white pictures or film, that's no problem! You can have a photo lab process your color negatives as black-and-white photos.
- Opt for photos without a lot of details. Closeup shots of people are a good choice, and remember that you don't have to color the entire photo. Groups of people and lots of background details will make a photo more difficult to color.
- If you're taking photos with black-and-white film, get close to your subject to eliminate unessential surroundings. If you're planning to hand-color the photo later, have the subject wear light colors and try to avoid using a flash, to give the most natural appearance.
- If possible, use a larger photo, such as an 8" x 10" print, for tinting. Coloring details in smaller prints can be a painstaking process. Have your enlargement devel-

oped at a good custom photo lab, where you can give instructions for any needed cropping as well as point out any areas that need to be lightened or darkened.

- When you have your print developed, select the best finish. If you're using photo oils, your print should have a matte finish. (If it doesn't, you'll have to use a precolor spray.) For hand-coloring pens, the print can have either a matte or a glossy finish.

photo oils

TINTING WITH PHOTO OILS

Photo oils and pencils have been used by hand colorists for many years to achieve striking archival-quality prints. The oils give you a lot of variety because you can mix colors, and if you make a mistake, it's easy to wipe off the oil and start over. However, oils are also messy and generally more time-consuming to use than hand-coloring pens.

In addition to the photo oils and pencils, you'll need cotton balls and cotton swabs, a vinyl eraser, a palette or plastic plate for mixing colors, toothpicks for applying fine details, drafting tape, and a finishing spray. To begin, tape your print to a flat surface with drafting tape (which lets you remove it later without damage). Then, use cotton swabs to apply the oils and cotton balls to blend the colors.

As you work, apply the base color first over the major subject area, such as the flesh color in a portrait. Next, use cotton swabs to clean up the borders, add color for highlights, and remove color for shadows. Be careful not to leave any clumps or buildup of oil on the print. Finally, add the details, working from the top of the photo down. Use a vinyl eraser to clean out areas such as eyes and teeth, and use pencils for detailed areas such as eyebrows and lips. Don't try to do *too* much—sometimes only a few highlights give the best results.

When you're finished, let the print dry for three days where it's dust free, such as in a box with a lid. When the print is dry, apply a finishing spray in a well-ventilated area to protect it, then let it dry a few hours more.

USING HAND-COLORING PENS

Hand-coloring pens are a fairly new, yet effective, method for easily tinting prints with a matte or glossy finish. These acid-free pens contain retouching dyes that are highly purified so they leave no surface residue on the print. Since the dyes penetrate the photo emulsion, a finishing spray isn't needed. Hand-coloring pens are quick and easy to use and there's no mess to clean up. However, it can be difficult to fix large mistakes, although a dye-remover pen

can be used to correct small mistakes.

To get started, purchase a starter kit that includes a set of hand-coloring pens in basic colors, premoistening solution, a dye-remover pen, a sponge, and cotton pads. You can also purchase additional pens in other colors if you want. Tape the print to a smooth work surface and prepare the moistening solution as directed. Premoistening the photo allows it to absorb the dyes better. Use the sponge from the starter kit to apply the moistening solution to the area of the print you're working on. The print should be tacky, not wet, to the touch.

The first time you use a pen, soften its tip by rubbing it on your tape border or the back of an unneeded photo. Then, start coloring! Color

By Ellen James, Orem, Utah. Scissors: Fiskars (Deckle); Stickers: Frances Meyer; Photo oils: Marshall Oils.

lightly with a circular motion—don't apply pressure. You can use retouching pens with fine tips for small details, such as eyes or eyebrows. If needed, remoisten the area to allow the color to soak in. As you color, blot any excess dye with cotton.

If you make a mistake, you can usually correct it immediately using a dye-remover pen. (If you'd rather start over, soak your print in a tray of water for one or two hours until the color is gone.) When you have finished coloring, simply let your print dry for a couple of hours. There's no need for any kind of finishing or protecting spray.

Hand coloring black-and-white photos is an enjoyable process that creates a lasting heirloom at the same time. Your scrapbook pages will have a dramatic new look as you showcase beautiful black-and-white prints—old and new.

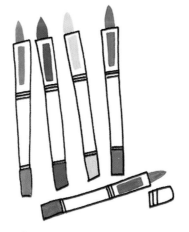

hand-coloring pens

Lettering

• • • • • • • • • • • Pens and Markers • • • • • • • • • • •

A PEN IS PERHAPS the simplest scrapbooking tool, but it's also one of the most versatile. There's an awful lot you can do with only a basic black, fine-tipped pen—not to mention all the possibilities once you add other pen colors and styles. Pens and markers can enhance your scrapbook pages through headlines, journaling, borders, and more. And by becoming familiar with the qualities to look for in a pen, you can be sure that the marks you make will last long into the future.

SELECTING THE BEST PENS FOR YOUR SCRAPBOOK

Not every pen or marker is good for your scrapbook. For example, some

By Becky Higgins, Peoria, Arizona. Pen: Zig Posterman; Stickers: Main Street Press. Ltd.

pens will smear if moisture comes into contact with them, and others will fade over time. When you're purchasing pens for your scrapbook, keep these qualities in mind:

Permanence • Always use permanent-ink pens in your scrapbook. This means that the ink is resistant to elements that can smear it, fade it, or otherwise remove it from the page, including water, light, chemicals, and so on. In addition to the label "permanent," look for pens marked as being waterproof, fade-resistant (also called "lightfast"), and chemical-resistant.

Archival Quality • Of course, you don't want the ink in your scrapbook to harm your photographs. So, look for archival-quality pens with ink that is photo-safe, nontoxic, and acid-free when dry.

Ink Type • The best type of permanent ink is pigment-based ink, as opposed to dye-based ink, which can fade significantly over time. However, just because an ink contains pigments doesn't mean that it's permanent. For example, watercolors that use pigments aren't permanent, and some pigment inks (especially fluorescent colors) aren't lightfast and will fade.

Ink Application • Another consideration is the behavior of the ink after it's been applied to the page. For example, some ink might seep or bleed through to the other side of the page, which is a concern if you add photos to both sides. Other ink might

run out into the paper, leaving you with fuzzy edges. In addition, some ink might take a long time to dry, increasing the chances of it smearing. The type of paper you use can also affect how the ink behaves. For example, ink is more likely to bleed on thinner papers (such as decorative papers) and to run more easily on textured papers.

Ease of Use • Finally, take into account how easy the pen is for you to write with. Do you like the way the ink flows out of the tip and the way it reacts to the amount of pressure you normally use when you write? Does the pen tip work well with your particular handwriting style? Before you purchase several colors of a specific pen, buy one and then try it out to see how you like the results. Many retail store displays have sample pens that you can try out before purchasing.

TYPES OF PENS AND MARKERS

Pens and markers that are suitable for scrapbooks come in all sorts of colors—from pastels to brights to metallics. You'll also find a large variety of pen tips and styles, each designed for a different purpose:

Fine-Tip • Fine-tip pens come in several different sizes, usually measured in millimeters (indicating the width of the tip), such as 0.5mm. These pens are perfect for caption text and journaling, as well as for outlining larger images and adding small details.

Bullet-Tip • Bullet-tip pens give you a bolder, wider stroke. The tip is still

create fun titles for your pages

rounded, which works well for writing large titles, coloring, and adding embellishments such as dots.

Chisel-Tip or Calligraphy • Chisel-tip pens—also called calligraphy pens—have a flattened tip that adds a little extra flair to your lettering. These pens come in various sizes and can create an elegant or casual look, depending on the angle you hold the pen at while writing.

Brush-Tip • Brush-tip pens have a flexible tip that makes them great for freehand lettering, as well as for coloring. You can create different line thicknesses from the same pen simply by applying different amounts of pressure. Brush-tip pens can also be used to ink rubber stamps.

Opaque or Paint • Opaque pens—or paint pens—are used for writing on darker-colored papers. You'll find several different tip sizes as well as a variety of colors including white, gold, and silver. (Be careful when first using your pen, as the ink can spurt out from a buildup of pressure.)

Gel-Based Roller • Roller-ball pens with a gel-based pigment ink are a fun way to add text and other fine details to your pages. Unlike standard roller-ball pens, gel-based rollers give you smooth, vibrant color until the last drop of ink is gone. (Some colors of gel ink can fade, so check with the manufacturer for more information.)

Dual-Tipped • Dual-tipped pens offer you the convenience of two pens in one. These pens use a combination of either two different tips, such as chisel and brush tips, or two different sizes of the same tip, such as small and large calligraphy tips. Each end of the pen has a separate tip and lid.

IDEAS FOR USING PENS AND MARKERS

There are lots of ways you can use pens and markers to enhance your scrapbook—even if you have only a handful of colors and styles to work with. Here are just a few ideas:

- Create fun titles and headings for your pages. With a little practice, you can become a creative lettering expert!

- Draw borders around individual photos or the entire page. Borders can be as simple as dashed lines or as complex as intertwined vines.

- Add small accents to the other elements on your page, such as stickers and die cuts. For example, you might draw "stitches" around a die cut for a quilted look, add dots to light-colored cardstock to create a sand texture, or draw in "movement" marks for a bee sticker.

- Color in images that you've printed, stamped, or traced on the page. If you're in a hurry, you can simply outline the images. However, since

pens and markers don't allow you to shade or blend colors very easily, you might consider using colored pencils or another medium if you do a lot of coloring.

- Draw embellishments—or even full-scale drawings—right on the page. For example, you can draw stars, hearts, pine trees—the sky's the limit!

Pens and markers may be among the most basic tools in a scrapbooker's supply bin, but they can create amazingly varied results.

By Lindsay Ostrom, Montrose, California. Paper: Cut-It-Out; Pens: EK Success, Zig Writers, Zig Clean Color, Zig Millennium, Zig Opaque Writers; Stickers: Stickopotamus and Mrs. Grossman's Borderlines; Jingle bells: local craft store.

• • • • • • • • • Pencils and Chalks • • • • • • • • • • •

PENS AND MARKERS give you a fast and easy way to add color to your scrapbook pages through lettering, coloring images, creating borders, and so on—but they're not your only option. You can also brighten up your pages with several other coloring tools, including colored pencils, watercolor pencils, and decorating chalks. Each of these tools creates its own look and allows you to blend and shade colors for a beautiful effect. They're especially useful for adding color to outline lettering and images, such as those from clip-art packages or rubber stamps.

COLORED PENCILS

Colored pencils have been around for a long time and come in an astounding variety of colors. They are easy to use, allowing you to blend and shade colors as well as add fine details. The colors are generally lighter and subtler than those from pens or markers, and they pick up the texture of the paper.

Try some of these techniques when you're using colored pencils:

- To lighten or darken the color, simply change the pressure you apply to the pencil—but don't press so hard that you damage the paper. You can also darken an area by coloring over it more than once with the same color.
- Layer different colors on top of each other to blend them and create new tones. Generally, apply the lightest color first, and then layer darker colors on top of it. However,

in some cases you might want to add white or another light color on top of an existing color to create a highlight.

- For a different look, try filling in a large area with hatching or cross-hatching. To create hatch marks, draw closely spaced parallel lines at an angle. If you want to add cross-hatching, draw additional lines over the first ones at an opposite angle (similar to crossing an X).
- Create a fun pattern by using a stipple technique, where you use the pencil to create dots of different colors. Place the dots close together for darker color and shading, and experiment with mixing different-colored dots.

WATERCOLOR PENCILS

If you like colored pencils but want some variety, try watercolor pencils. These pencils can be used just like colored pencils, but by adding a little water you can also blend or create softer shades, or make even bolder colors. There are four different ways you can use watercolor pencils in your scrapbook:

- The basic method is simply to draw and color on the page with the dry watercolor pencils, as you would with any regular colored pencil.
- To create softer shades, first color with the pencils on the page as you normally would. Then, use a damp brush or cotton swab to blend any of the colors. Make sure the brush or swab doesn't have too much

Tips for Applying Color

KEEP THESE TIPS IN MIND as you apply color to your scrapbook pages—no matter which tool you use:

- Start with the lightest color and then add darker colors in layers.
- Use darker shades of a color for shadows instead of black. For example, a shadowed area of a red object might be a deep red or purple.
- Leave lighter areas for highlights in spots where a light source (the sun or a lamp) might hit the object.
- Apply your strokes in the same direction to provide an even, uniform look. For example, use a circular motion for all decorating chalks, and keep your colored pencil marks all side by side.
- Select color combinations that help enhance the theme and mood of your page. Also, when you're adding titles and other text, choose a color with enough contrast to the background so the text is easy to read.

water in it or the paper might warp. You can layer colors and then use water to blend them together. After allowing the colors to dry, you can use the dry pencils to add any further detail on top.

- If you want to create bold, vivid lines, dip the pencil tip in water (or apply water to the tip with a damp brush), then draw on your page.
- You can create your own palette of soft colors by rubbing selected pencils on a separate piece of heavier paper. Then, add a few drops of water to each colored area and use a brush to transfer the color to your page.

If you're using watercolor pencils with a rubber-stamped image, make sure the image has been stamped with pigment ink (as opposed to water-based ink), so any water added with the pencils doesn't cause the stamp ink to run. In addition, you might want to protect your finished work from moisture by using an acid-free spray fixative or sealer before adding any photos.

DECORATING CHALKS

Decorating chalks (also called pastels) are a fast and fun way to add color to your scrapbook pages. Decorating chalks come in many colors, and they blend together beautifully. Chalks are one of the fastest methods for coloring a large area, but they're not so good for adding fine details.

To apply decorating chalks to your page, you can use a small sponge-tipped tool (similar to an eye shadow applicator), a cotton swab, or even your fingertips. Use a circular motion to apply the colors, and do the lighter colors first. You can layer colors on top of each other and then blend them, or you can reapply the same color to increase the intensity. Decorating chalks can easily smear and smudge, so be careful as you're applying them. (You can purchase a special eraser for removing chalk smudges.) When you're finished, protect your page with an acid-free spray fixative to prevent further smearing. (Spray the page before adding your photos.)

When you are looking for a way to brighten your scrapbook with a little extra color, don't forget about tools such as pencils and chalks. They're a nice change from pens and markers, and they create stunning results!

By Becky Higgins, Peoria, Arizona. Pen: Zig Writer; Pencils: Prisma Color; Stickers: Mrs. Grossman's.

By Becky Higgins, Peoria, Arizona. Paper: Provo Craft; Pens: Zig Writer (black outline) and Prisma Color pencil (white and brown fill).

Lettering Styles

THE WORDS IN YOUR scrapbook can have a powerful impact, not only in what they say but also in how they look. Lettering helps convey the personality of a page—from fun and spunky to elegant and graceful to serious and thoughtful.

LETTERING STYLES

There are hundreds of different lettering styles available, from simple printing to elaborate calligraphy. Each style can be defined by a variety of characteristics, including the following:

Form and Structure • A lettering style is partially determined by how the letters in each word are formed. For example, the individual letters within each word might be written separately (as in printing), or they might be connected together (as in cursive writing). In addition, styles can vary by the height of the waist in each letter (for example, the crossbar of an A), as well as by the length of descending segments on letters such as *g* and *y*.

Shape • Letters can suggest a certain mood simply by their shape. For example, rounded letters and long, sweeping strokes contribute to a softer, elegant feeling, while more defined, pointed letters convey a modern, straightforward approach.

Serifs • Many lettering styles have serifs—small markings at the end of each letter stroke. (The main text in this book is serif.) Serifs are commonly short crossbars, but they can also be dots, hearts, or other embellishments in a variety of sizes and shapes. Of course, letters don't have to have any serifs at all, in which case they are called *sans-serif* typefaces. (The captions and headings in this book are sans-serif.)

Weight • Letters can be made up of fine lines or broad strokes. Thicker letters, often referred to as *block letters*, might be filled in with a solid color or pattern, or simply be left in outline form.

Case • Lettering styles with all uppercase letters are frequently used for titles and other areas of the page to which you want to draw attention. Styles with all lowercase letters give the writing a casual, even shy, voice. Most frequently, writing is a mixture of uppercase and lowercase letters.

TECHNIQUES FOR CREATING LETTERING

When you want to add text to your scrapbook pages, you not only have to decide what style of lettering to use, you also have to determine *how* you'll actually create the lettering. There are many different lettering techniques, and with each one you can create a wide range of styles and looks. Here are a few ideas:

Freehand • Text that you write with your own hand is the most personalized lettering as well as the most cherished. Use your own natural handwriting or learn a technique such as block lettering or calligraphy to add some variety to your pages. The best way to improve your hand-lettering skills is to practice!

Stencils • Many alphabet stencils and templates are available that can help you easily put fun lettering in your scrapbook. All you have to do is trace the letters directly on the page or on cardstock, which you then cut out. Stencils usually come in some form of block letters, although you can find a variety of lettering styles.

Computer Fonts • If you have a computer and printer, you have access to hundreds of different font styles.

By Rachel Lewis, Hyrum, Utah. Pens: Zig Clean Color; Scissors: Fiskars(Mini-Pinking); Stickers: Melissa Neufeld.

By Becky Higgins, Peoria, Arizona. The headlines on this spread use a triangular fill-in lettering that has spiral embellishments.

Computer fonts are a popular method for adding unique lettering to scrapbook pages because they're so easy to use and there are so many choices available. If your album pages are removable and fit in your printer, you can print the text right on your scrapbook page (before you put any photos or stickers on). Or, you can print on coordinating cardstock and then cut out the text to glue on your page.

Rubber Stamps • Letters created with rubber stamps work especially well for initial capitals and drop caps (initial letters that descend two or three lines into the ensuing paragraph). You can also find rubber stamps that contain entire words or phrases already formatted.

Die Cuts • If you like the block letter format created by stencils, but don't like taking the time to cut out each individual letter, take a look at die-cut letters. You can purchase precut letters or quickly create your own if you have access to a die-cutting machine. Because die-cut letters are fairly large, they're most often used for page titles.

Stickers • Alphabet stickers are another fun way to add lettering to your scrapbook pages. Stickers are great for titles, initial capitals, and drop caps.

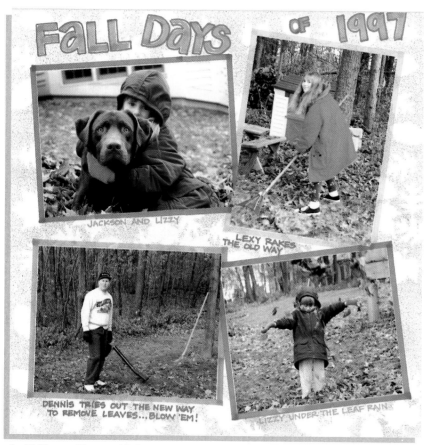

FALL DAYS OF 1997

JACKSON AND LIZZY

LEXY RAKES
THE OLD WAY

DENNIS TRIES OUT THE NEW WAY
TO REMOVE LEAVES...BLOW 'EM!

LIZZY UNDER THE LEAF RAIN

By Jill Rinner, Okemos, Michigan. Pens: Studio 2, Printworks; Punch: Family Treasures.

GENERAL LETTERING TIPS

The best tip for creating better lettering is to practice! Here are some other tips so you get the best results.

- Select a lettering style that's appropriate for your overall page theme. For example, you probably wouldn't want to have flowing script letters on a football page. Some lettering styles fit a very specific theme (such as *winter* or *baby*), while others are more neutral.

- Consider the length of the text when choosing a style. An uppercase block lettering style might work great for a bold headline but would be difficult to read if it were used for a long paragraph of journaling.

- Try to avoid having too many different lettering styles on the same page, since this can be confusing and distract from your photos.

- Remember that your lettering does not always have to appear in a straight line—sometimes it's fun to have headlines that create a wave or zigzag look. You can also try staggering or alternately tilting letters.

- Before you draw or glue down the first letter, make sure there's room for the entire word or phrase in the style you've selected.

- If you're using a stencil to trace and cut letters from coordinating cardstock, turn the stencil over and trace the letters backward. After cutting out the letters, turn them over so the pencil marks are on the back and the letters appear correctly. This eliminates the need to erase any stray pencil marks.

- When you're creating freehand lettering, pencil in the letters on your page before outlining them with a permanent pen.

LETTERING FOR TITLES AND HEADLINES

Titles and headlines allow great creativity when it comes to lettering in your scrapbook. Because titles are generally only one or two words long and are the largest text on the page, you can use more elaborate lettering styles than you would for smaller captions and journaling passages. In addition, you have a lot of choices of specific theme-oriented lettering styles that usually work best as page titles.

If your scrapbook page has a title (and not every page needs one), make sure that it's large enough to grab attention but not so bold that it overpowers your photographs. Page titles are commonly positioned at the top of the page, although they can also be placed down one side or even across the bottom. All of the lettering techniques described above work well for titles and headlines.

Here are a few freehand lettering styles you might try for titles:

Serif Lettering • One of the easiest types of freehand lettering to create is a simple serif style. Just print the title in fairly neat handwriting, and then add a short line, dot, heart, square, or another embellishment to the end point of each stroke. For a letter without a serif, such as an *o*, you can add an ornament to the top edge (either centered or slightly off-center).

Outlined Lettering • Another easy lettering style to create is outlined lettering. First, print the word using a fairly thick marker, with the letters fairly close together. (You can also write the word in cursive if you want.) Then, use a finer-tipped pen to outline the entire word. You can outline the word with the same color, or you can even layer several different colors.

Block Lettering • To create titles with block lettering, first write the word or words in pencil, making sure you leave enough space between each letter for the extra thickness. Then, create an outline of each letter. Depending on how thick you want the letters, you can simply add a double line along one side of

the letters, or you can draw a line all the way around the original letter. Now, you can fill in the letters with a solid color or a pattern. Add any extras that you want, such as "caps" of snow for winter lettering, or a "frosting" of dots and lines (using an opaque or paint pen).

Fill-in Lettering • This lettering style is a fun way to personalize your writing to match your page theme. To create fill-in lettering, first print the word in pencil in all uppercase letters. Then, outline a block around the left vertical stroke in each letter. The block might

be drawn completely around the original letter stroke, or it might be drawn using the original letter stroke as the right edge. For a letter such as O, draw a curved line inside the left side of the letter. Outline the final letters with a permanent pen, erase any pencil marks, and then fill in the space with a solid color or pattern. The possibilities for what you can add inside the letters are endless! Add serifs to the ends of each stroke to finish off the lettering.

A slight variation of fill-in lettering is to write the word in mixed case (uppercase for the first letter of

Stickers decorate these hand-drawn letters. By Gaylene Steinbach, Lincoln, Nebraska. Stickers: Mrs. Grossman's; Die Cuts: Ellison; Christmas card: Plus Mark.

each word, with the rest of the letters lowercase). Then, instead of widening just the left edge of each letter, block every major vertical stroke to make the letters wider (similar to block letters), but still leave some parts of the letters with the original single thickness. Finally, fill in the spaces created with a pattern or solid color.

LETTERING FOR INITIAL CAPITALS

A fast way to spruce up your page lettering is to create drop caps or ornamental initial capitals.

Drop Caps • Drop caps are often in a more elaborate style than the paragraph text. If you don't want to draw the letter freehand, use a sticker, rubber stamp, or computer font, which gives you an instant letter and also adds contrast to the paragraph text.

Ornamental Initial Capitals • Ornamental initial capitals can help you save space with a long page title but still enhance your theme. With this type of lettering, the first letter of the first word in your title (or the first letter of each main word) is capitalized and uses a different lettering style from the rest of the letters. For example, the capital letters might have a vine and flowers entwined around them for a "May Pole" heading, or they might be block letters decorated with black spots for a "Visit to the Farm" title. Initial capitals are also a fun way to spruce up short photo captions.

By Channa Brewer, Mesa, Arizona. Paper: The Paper Patch; Pens: Zig Clean Color; Stickers: Mrs. Grossman's; Die Cuts: Ellison (sun), Accu-Cut (fern); Corner rounder: Uchida.

By Deanna Lambson, Sandy, Utah. Paper: D.O.T.S.; Alphabet stickers: Making Memories.

LETTERING FOR CAPTIONS AND JOURNALING PASSAGES

The writing for captions and journaling passages is usually relatively small (especially compared to page titles), so make sure that the text is easy to read. Here are a few tips for creating lettering for captions and journaling:

- Try to stay away from fancy script fonts, uppercase letters, and other lettering styles that are difficult to read in large amounts and smaller sizes.
- The best lettering techniques for captions and journaling passages are freehand writing (printing or cursive) and computer fonts. Stickers, stamps, and die cuts tend to be too large.

- If you're writing several lines of text by hand, lightly pencil in ruler lines first to help you keep the letters straight. After writing with a permanent pen, you can remove the pencil lines with a good eraser.
- Try writing your captions around the shape of the photo or even around the page border.
- You can use special rubber stamps for photo journaling that help you record details for a variety of different photos and give you lines to write on at the same time.
- If you use computer fonts for most of your captions and journaling, make an effort to include at least a few passages in your own handwriting somewhere in your scrapbook. Your handwriting is a unique expression of you! (Think how much you appreciate handwritten notes from your grandparents or great-grandparents.)

From large page titles to small photo captions, lettering helps to enhance the personality of your scrapbook pages. It's good to experiment and practice with different lettering styles and techniques. You'll be a lettering expert before you know it!

Practice, Practice!

THE BEST WAY TO BECOME BETTER at lettering—especially freehand lettering—is to spend lots of time practicing. Get out a stack of scratch paper and your pens, and start writing! Here are some ideas:

- Write your name several times in the same lettering style to get a feel for it. You can also write phrases such as "The quick brown fox jumps over the lazy dog." Also, practice writing the numbers from 1 to 10.

- Try writing the same word using different types of pen tips to see which you like best.

- Experiment with raising or lowering the waist of the letters to see what different looks you can create. (The waist is the area where an A is crossed or where the circle portion of a P intersects the vertical stem.)

- Use a ruler to help you position letters in a straight line.

- Try placing the letters in a word closer together or farther apart to see the different effects you can create.

- Before you draw the first letter on a page, write the word on a piece of scratch paper so you know how much room it will take up.

Rubber Stamps

• • • • • • • • • Rubber-Stamp Style • • • • • • • • •

RUBBER-STAMPING has been around for years as a fun and creative hobby in its own right, but it also makes a terrific partner with scrapbooking. Stamps give you a fast and easy way to enhance your scrapbook, and with the huge selection of stamp sizes and styles available, you're sure to find one that's just perfect for each page. (One of the neat things about stamps is that they become a permanent part of your scrapbook page, so you don't have to worry about them falling off!)

TYPES OF RUBBER STAMPS

Rubber stamps come in an unbelievable variety of styles to suit every personal taste. You can find stamps for practically any occasion, season, or holiday—in styles ranging from Victorian to cute and whimsical to contemporary and modern. Here are some specific types of stamps that work well in scrapbooks:

Image Stamps • Image stamps range from under an inch to several inches in size. Most create only an outline, which you can color in if you want after stamping. Other stamps are more solid and create a silhouette-type image in the ink color you've selected. (Some stamps use a combination of outline and solid areas.) Image stamps are a great way to fill in empty space on your scrapbook page while enhancing your theme.

Mini Stamps • Mini stamps are a type of image stamp and create a picture, shape, or other design on your page. These stamps are usually under an inch in size and often come in sets of related images and shapes.

Frame Stamps • Some of the largest stamps available are frame stamps, which create a border around a rectangular, square, or oval area. As with other stamps, you'll find a large variety of styles, and you can place either a photo or text inside the frame area. If you want to frame a photo, you can stamp right on your page and then crop the photo to match the inside of the frame shape. (To make this easier, create a template by stamping on a piece of cardstock and cutting out the center.) Or, you can cut out the center of the stamped frame on the page and then mount the photo on the underside of the page. Another option is to stamp the frame on a separate piece of cardstock, cut it out, and mount it over your photo.

By Karen Kehoe, Yorba Linda, California. Rubber Stamp: Stampendous (bricks); Other: magazine cutouts (roses).

By Rosemary Bluhm, Someret, California. Paper: Northern Spy. Rubber Stamps: Northern Spy.

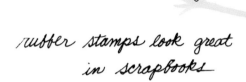

rubber stamps look great in scrapbooks

Photo Corner Stamps • A fairly new type of stamp is a photo corner stamp, which gives you a quick method for sprucing up your photos. You can stamp the photo corners on adhesive paper, cut them out, and stick them in place, or you can stamp directly on the page (after tracing where you want the photo placed) and cut slits along the inside edge to slip the photos under.

Journaling Stamps • If you need a little help recording the important details for the photos on a page, try a journaling stamp. These stamps provide an area for jotting down names, dates, and other memories. Many of the stamps include blank lines that you can write on after stamping. Some other stamp designs are "thought bubbles" or banners that make a fun addition to your pages.

Alphabet Stamps • Alphabet lettering stamps come in a wide assortment of sizes and styles. You can purchase complete alphabet sets or individual letters; usually, the individual stamps are larger capital letters. Alphabet stamps are a neat way to create page titles and headlines.

BASIC STAMPING TIPS AND TECHNIQUES

For the best results from the combination of rubber stamps and scrapbooks:

• Purchase stamps that have the rubber edges trimmed close to the raised image and are cut deep enough to make a good impression. Most stamps are mounted on wood, but you can also find quality foam-mounted stamps.

• Look for pads with pigment ink (as opposed to dye-ink pads). Pigment ink is permanent.

• When you're applying ink to your stamp, tap the stamp on the pad several times, without applying too much pressure. If you grind the stamp into the pad, the ink can spread unevenly and also transfer to the edges of the design. If you have a raised ink pad that's smaller than the stamp, turn the stamp over and press the ink pad over the entire design.

• Before you actually stamp the image on your scrapbook page, practice stamping it a few times on a piece of scratch paper—especially if it's a new stamp. This helps you get a feel for how much ink you need to apply to the stamp and reveals any areas that might need a little extra pressure.

• To create the best impression after inking the stamp, place the stamp firmly in place on the paper. Press straight down on the stamp—don't rock it back and forth. For large stamps, make sure you apply pressure over the entire design; try laying one hand facedown over the stamp and then applying pressure with the other hand. Lift the stamp straight up to avoid smearing or smudging.

• Take care of your stamps by keeping them clean. Clean the stamps each time you change ink colors and before you put them away at the end of a project. You can clean stamps with damp paper towels, paint pads (which have small fingerlike fibers and are commonly used to apply paint), a specific stamp cleaning solution, or even baby wipes (make sure they're not alcohol-based wipes, which can dry the rubber). Some colors of ink might stain the rubber—this is normal and shouldn't affect any new images you stamp.

• When you've finished using your stamps, store them facedown and away from sun or high temperatures.

Rubber stamps are a versatile scrapbooking tool that can enhance any scrapbook page. The sections in the next few pages highlight some of the stamping techniques you can use to get the most out of your stamp collection, such as embossing and masking. The more you practice stamping, the better you'll become at getting crisp, clear images—and you just might find yourself addicted to a new hobby!

• • • • • • • • Rubber-Stamp Embossing • • • • • • •

EMBOSSING IS ONE OF the most popular—and beautiful—techniques you can use with rubber stamps. The raised surface of embossed images adds texture and polish to your scrapbook pages. The term *embossing* can actually refer to two different techniques—thermal embossing, which raises the stamp ink, and dry embossing, which raises the surface of the paper.

THERMAL EMBOSSING

Thermal (or heat) embossing adds an elegant touch to your stamped images by giving the ink a shiny, raised appearance—similar to what you might see on a professional business card. Thermal embossing involves two basic products: ink and embossing powder.

Ink • The two best types of ink for thermal embossing are pigment ink and embossing ink. Both types remain wet long enough for the embossing powder to stick to them, and both come in a wide variety of colors. (Dye ink dries too quickly for embossing to work successfully.) Pigment ink can be used also for regular stamping and lettering, while embossing ink is designed for thermal embossing only and is commonly found in a clear color. You can find both types of ink in either pads or markers; either form can be used for embossing.

Embossing Powder • Embossing powder is purchased in small jars and comes in many different colors, including metallic colors such as gold and silver. Clear embossing powder is a favorite choice for embossing over colored inks, since the

ink color shows through the embossing. Colored and metallic embossing powders can be embossed over similarly colored ink or clear embossing ink.

HOW TO THERMAL EMBOSS AN IMAGE

To create a thermal-embossed image in your scrapbook, follow these steps:

By Leslie Randle, Okemos, Michigan. Embossing pen: Tsukineko; Rubber Stamps: Printworks (alphabet and block), Toomuchfun (baby shoes); Frostwhite pad: Colorbox.

1. Lay a piece of scratch paper or an open file folder on your work surface to catch the extra powder.
2. Ink the stamp that you want to use with an ink pad or marker. Then, stamp the image where you want it on the page. (You can also use an embossing marker to write or draw directly on the scrapbook page without using a stamp at all.)
3. Pour embossing powder liberally over the stamped ink while it's still wet.

(You'll be able to save any unused powder.) After covering the inked area, tip the page over your scratch paper to pour off the excess powder. You can use a fine brush if needed to remove any stray powder particles.

4. Now you're ready to melt the powder with a heat source. If you have one available, use an embossing heat gun (purchased at craft or stamp stores) and hold it a few inches above the image, slowly moving it back and forth. (Make sure you carefully read and follow the instructions from the heat gun manufacturer.) If you don't have an embossing heat tool, you can use another heat source, such as the top of a toaster oven. (Also, check the directions on the jar for suggestions from the manufacturer of the embossing powder.) A hair dryer does *not* work for embossing because it doesn't get hot enough and simply blows the powder away. Hold the paper above the heat source and move it back and forth slowly to melt the powder evenly (being careful not to burn your fingers). Don't get the page too close to the heat source or you might scorch the paper. When the powder is melted, it will have a shiny, raised appearance.

5. Finally, save your unused powder by picking up the paper or folder containing the excess powder by the edges, folding it to create a funnel, and pouring the powder back into the original jar.

   If you missed any spots in the image, you can use an embossing pen

By Leslie Randle, Okemos, Michigan. Rubber Stamps: Stampington & Company (snowman and snowman frames); Posh Impressions (crystal flake); Rubber Stampede (other crystal flake); Fonts: Chunky, Fontastic!, D.J. Inkers; Frost white pad: Colorbox.

to reink that section, then add the embossing powder and heat it again. Experiment with different colors of ink and powder to see what combinations you like best. You can also try embossing with several powder colors on the same image (tapping off the excess of each color before adding a new color).

DRY EMBOSSING

Another type of embossing is dry embossing, which makes the actual paper "pop up," rather than simply the ink. To create this type of embossing, you need a brass stencil, a matching rubber stamp (if desired), an embossing stylus, and a light table (or a similar source of backlighting). Dry embossing can be done with only a brass stencil on an unprinted area of the page, or it can be done with a matching stamp and stencil set, so the entire stamped image is raised off the page.

Follow these steps to create a dry-embossed image:

1. If you have a matching stamp for your stencil (you can still emboss without a matching stamp), first stamp the image where you want it on the scrapbook page. Because the embossing will outline the overall shape of the image, you don't have to ink the entire stamp if you don't want to. (Leaving portions of a stamp blank is easiest if you're inking the stamp with markers rather than a pad.)

2. Place the brass stencil on the light box with the design facedown. Then, lay the paper facedown on top of the stencil, matching up the stamped image (if any) with the stencil. If you don't have a stamped image, position the part of the page you want to emboss over the stencil. You can also create a *debossed* image, where the paper is recessed instead of raised, by laying the page faceup over the stencil.

3. Use the stylus to trace over the stencil, pushing the paper slightly through the open sections of the stencil. You don't have to emboss the entire stencil design—simply press over the sections you want. If you're working with a border or frame design, you can stretch the design to fit a certain area by embossing each corner separately and then embossing the edges in small sections, repositioning and realigning the stencil until all the edges are filled in.

Embossing can turn your ordinary scrapbook pages into elegant works of art. And the best part is that it only takes a minute or two to create this stunning look.

•••••••••• Coloring and Masking ••••••••••

RUBBER STAMPS ARE surprisingly versatile, allowing you to create a variety of different looks with only one or two stamps. For example, you can color in a stamped image any number of ways, stamp just a portion of an image, or combine stamps to create a new scene (with a technique called *masking*). With a little experimentation and practice, you'll be amazed at how much mileage you can get out of a single stamp.

COLORING
Generally, a stamped image appears in one color—whatever color of ink you

By Dee Gruenig, Irvine, California. Paper: Hot Off The Press (lattice); Rubber Stamps: Posh Impressions. Frame was stamped on glossy paper and colored in with a pen.

happened to use. But there are lots of ways you can add multiple colors to the stamped images on your pages. Here are a few ideas:

Watercolors • Watercolors are a fast way to color in your images after they've been stamped, giving them a soft, painted look. To use this technique, you'll need dye-based ink from a pad or marker (brush markers work well) and a good-quality round brush. First, stamp the image on the page using permanent pigment ink. Then, create your own watercolor palette using a piece of plastic such as the lid from a margarine tub. If you're using a watercolor (dye-based) ink pad, press the pad onto the plastic to transfer some of the ink. If you're using dye-based markers, scribble a few lines on the plastic; the ink might bead up, which is normal. Moisten the brush slightly and pick up some of the ink from the plastic, then paint your image. Be careful that you don't get too much water in the brush or the color will become diluted and your paper might warp.

Brush Markers • Brush markers are a quick method for stamping several colors at the same time. These markers come in a huge variety of colors and are usually dye-based (although you can also use pigment markers). Rather than using a pad to ink your stamp, turn the stamp

over and color directly on the stamp with the markers. Start with the lightest color to keep your pen tips clean. You can color only those portions that you want to stamp, and if you make a mistake, use a moistened cotton swab to wipe the color off. After applying all the color, "huff" on the stamp (as if you were cleaning a pair of eyeglasses) to remoisten the ink. Then stamp the image on the page. You can also spray the inked stamp with a very fine mist of water before stamping to dilute and blend the colors.

Regular Stamp Ink • You can create images in varying shades by simply not reinking the stamp. Ink your stamp once with your favorite pigment ink (which comes in lots of colors) and start stamping. Each time you stamp without reinking, the image becomes lighter, creating a ghost appearance. This is a great way to add shadows or the feeling of motion to your page. If you want only one light image on the page (rather than several successively lighter images), stamp the image on a piece of scratch paper one or two times to remove some of the ink before stamping on your scrapbook page.

Other Coloring Tools • Several other tools can be used to color in the images you've stamped on a page. For example, you can use colored pencils, watercolor pencils, or decorating chalks. See page 104 for more information about each of these techniques.

With so many coloring options to choose from, your stamped images can

1

2

3

4

5

easily match and enhance your scrapbook pages. Keep in mind, however, that dye-based ink (such as ink used for watercolors and many brush markers) is not as permanent as pigment ink, so it is more likely to fade over time.

MASKING

If you have two or three stamps that coordinate well, you can overlap them to create a scene with a sense of depth. This is done with a technique called masking, where you temporarily cover up and protect a stamped image in order to stamp another image that will seem to be behind it. For example, you might combine a stamp of trees or mountains with a tent stamp to create a campground scene. Follow these steps to use masking with your stamps:

1. Select the stamps that you want to overlap and determine which stamp will be in the background and which will be in the foreground. The stamp in the foreground will show the complete image, while any stamps in the background will be partially covered. Plan a tentative positioning of the stamps on your page. Keep in mind that in creating a realistic appearance of depth, background items are usually placed higher up on the page to seem farther away, while foreground items are placed lower on the page.

2. Begin with the *foreground* image and stamp it in the position you want on your page. Then, stamp the same image on a sticky note or another piece of thin scratch paper (such as typewriter paper). If you stamp on a sticky note, make sure that at least part of the image is at the top where the strip of adhesive is located.

3. Cut the image out from the sticky note or scratch paper to create the mask. For the most convincing effect, cut closely along the *inside* edge of the stamped lines. If the image is large and you plan to overlap a second stamp on only one side, you need to cut out the image only along that side. If you're using a stamped image such as a frame or window and want to have a second image appear inside of it, cut out the center section of the mask. (This is sometimes called a *reverse mask*.)

4. Place the mask directly on top of the stamped image on the scrapbook page. If necessary, use a temporary adhesive to hold the mask in place. (You might be able to hold larger masks with your free hand.) Now, ink the back-

ground stamp and stamp it on the page so that it's positioned partially—or completely—over the mask that's protecting the first stamped image.

5. After stamping, remove the mask and you'll end up with one of the images appearing to be behind the other. Continue to mask and stamp any other images to complete your picture. You can even use the same stamp as both your foreground and background image (for example, to create a forest of trees).

If you're just getting started with your rubber-stamp collection, look for stamps that can be used individually or combined with other stamps to create fun scenes. Background stamps, such as trees or fences, are especially useful, since they can add life and dimension to many other stamps. As you experiment with different ways to color and position your stamps, you'll discover new looks that will make a great addition to any scrapbook page.

• • • • • • • • Lettering and Sponging • • • • • • • •

When you combine rubber-stamping with scrapbooking, you open up a whole new range of options for enhancing your scrapbook pages. In addition to stamping pictures on your pages, you can use stamps to create page headings and titles. You can also create unique background designs for your pages using stamping supplies and a technique called *sponging*. These techniques give you even more choices for adding a little variety and texture to your scrapbook.

By Sherril Watts. Rubber Stamps: Raindrops on Roses (star); Cloud Stencil: Sherril's own design.

LETTERING

Alphabet and number stamps come in many different styles and sizes. While these stamps are generally too large for creating captions or journaling passages, they're a neat alternative for creating larger page titles. Alphabet and number stamps also work great in ABC albums (see page 38). For example, if you have several different B stamps, you can scatter them throughout your B page to fill up empty space and reinforce the theme.

One of the drawbacks to alphabet and number stamps is that they can be difficult to line up and space properly. This is often due to the fact that the wood mount makes it hard to tell precisely where the stamp image will hit the page. Here are a few different techniques you can use to avoid this problem:

- Stagger or tilt the letters slightly so it doesn't matter if they don't exactly line up. For example, you can position every other letter a little higher, or you can alternate tilting the letters to the right or left.
- Use a ruler to pencil in a line on your page. Stamp the letters along the line, and then erase any pencil marks.
- Cut out from cardstock small squares that are slightly larger than the letters you want to stamp. For example, if your stamp letters are 1″ tall, cut out squares approximately 1.5″ wide and tall. Then, stamp each letter on a separate square and arrange the squares on your scrapbook page.
- Use a stamp positioner to place the stamps right where you want them. This handy tool comes in a few different styles (and you can also make your own), but they all work the same in providing a precise way to line up your stamps.

SPONGING AND STENCILING

Sponging and stenciling are techniques frequently associated with rubber-stamping. To use these techniques, simply dab a sponge in ink or paint and then tap the sponge lightly on the page. You can sponge with stencils to create specific images, or you can sponge directly on the page to create background designs for other images.

Sponging works with pigment- and dye-based inks as well as with acid-free paper paint and acrylic paint. You can use many types of sponges to transfer the ink or paint to your page. Different densities of sponges will give you different results and textures, and you can also experiment with materials such as paper towels, netting, burlap, and so on. For the best results, use a rounded sponge that doesn't have definite edges and corners; otherwise, the edge marks may show up in the ink you sponge on the page. For sponges such as cosmetic wedge sponges, try rounding

By Lisa Bearnson, Orem, Utah. Stickers: Stickopotamus; Rubber Stamps: D.J. Inkers.

the corners and clipping the edges to reduce the edge marks.

Here are a few ideas for sponging in your scrapbook:

- Add background texture by lightly sponging color right on the page—either before or after you stamp other images. If you want to protect a previously stamped image from the sponging texture, create a mask to cover it while you sponge. (See page 117 for more information on masking.)

- Use a sponge and stencil to transfer an image or border to your scrapbook page. You can find full-page stencils that are designed for creating background patterns, as well as stencils with images, photo frames, lettering, and so on. Position the area of the stencil that you want to use over your page, dab your sponge in ink or paint, and then sponge the color through the hole in the stencil.

- Create your own small stencil using a paper punch. Punch a shape through a small piece of cardstock, and then use that cardstock as a stencil to sponge the shape as many times as you want on the page. This is a great way to add small designs such as stars or snowflakes across your page.

- Use a *reverse stencil* to create an image on your page. This technique is commonly used to add designs such as clouds and stars to a background. First, cut out the shape you want from a piece of cardstock. Position the cutout cardstock shape on the page and sponge color around its edges. When you remove the cardstock, the shape of the image remains on the page.

Sponging and lettering are just two more ways for you to create beautiful designs in your scrapbook. By teaming up rubber-stamping and scrapbooking, you'll never run out of possibilities for unique scrapbook pages.

Using a Stamp Positioner

A STAMP POSITIONER IS EXTREMELY HELPFUL in making sure your stamped images end up exactly where you want them. The positioner is an L-shaped tool (although some look more like a T-square). It is generally at least 0.5″ thick and is often made out of acrylic. In addition to the positioner, you also need a thin, clear acrylic square (which is commonly included with the positioner) or a piece of tracing paper.

To use a stamp positioner, follow these steps:

1. Place the positioner on a flat surface and align the acrylic square or a square piece of tracing paper inside the corner.

2. Ink the stamp you want to use and align it in the same corner of the positioner (making sure the wood mount is flush with both sides of the positioner). Press the stamp down to create an image in the corner of the acrylic square or tracing paper.

3. Next, place the stamped acrylic square or piece of tracing paper over your scrapbook page, positioning it where you want the image to appear. (The clear acrylic or tracing paper lets you see any images already on the page.)

4. Move the positioner back to the corner of the acrylic square or tracing paper so both edges are aligned.

5. Carefully remove the acrylic square or tracing paper, keeping the positioner in place on the scrapbook page. (You can clean the square with water to reuse it later.)

6. Ink your stamp again and align it in the corner of the positioner, just as you did when making the first image. Stamp the image on the page, and when you remove the positioner and stamp, your image will be in the perfect position!

Journaling

• • • Words Are the Heart of Documentation • • •

PHOTOGRAPHS CAN CAPTURE and record many memories, but those memories aren't complete without words to fill in the details. That's why journaling in your scrapbook—adding text to describe the photos—is so important. Journaling allows you to tell the stories behind the pictures, record important facts and dates, and share memories that might otherwise be forgotten. Your stories and memories are some of the best things you can hand down to your children and grandchildren.

By Brenda Hall, Yuma, Arizona. Paper: D.O.T.S.; Scissors: Family Treasures (Antique Elegance); Stickers: Stickopotamus; Other: Embossed card by Making Memories; Book: Brenda's own design.

TIPS FOR EASIER JOURNALING

At times the thought of trying to write and record every detail and memory in your scrapbook can be overwhelming. Here are a few tips to make the journaling process easier and more enjoyable:

• Don't worry if you don't have perfect penmanship. Your handwriting is an important expression of your personality and makes an especially nice touch in a scrapbook. You want your writing to be legible, but remember that *what* you write is much more meaningful than the appearance of the letters. If you want, you can use a computer to print out some of your journaling passages.

• Jot down notes on your calendar or a notepad to help you remember important details as they happen. If you're working with a large collection of older photos, take the time initially to record any details you can on the backs of the photographs (using a photo marking pencil). The longer you wait to write things down, the more you're likely to forget.

• Stick with the basics. Don't try to tell your life story on one page. Instead, focus on one or two simple aspects—what your child's favorite ice-cream flavor is, what you liked best about your vacation, how you feel when it rains, and so on.

• Don't feel that you have to add a clever caption to every photograph —there's a difference between captions and journaling. Captions and "thought bubbles" can be a fun way to enhance your photographs, but they often don't convey the important journaling details (who, what, when, where, and why) or tell the story behind the photos. Of course, there's nothing wrong with adding clever captions to your photos— and you might find that they're easier to write after getting the general details down on the page.

ADDING JOURNALING TO YOUR SCRAPBOOK

Journaling can appear practically anywhere on a scrapbook page—and there's no rule that says it always has to be in straight lines. Some photographs warrant more journaling than others. You might even have a scrapbook page that contains nothing *but* journaling for photographs on the facing page. Here are a few tips and ideas for adding journaling to your scrapbook pages:

• When you write in your scrapbook, use a quality pen that is permanent and waterproof (see page 102 for more information on pens). If you use your computer to print journaling directly on the page, do so *before* adding any photographs or other page accents. If the ink from your printer isn't permanent, you can photocopy the printed text and put the copy on your page.

- You can add text beneath each photo that identifies who is in the picture and explains any other details. This caption can also appear above or next to the photo. As mentioned earlier, if you already have the journaling information on the page, your captions might be clever sayings or titles that add a touch of personality to the page.
- If there's a story to tell behind the pictures, write a paragraph that describes the events in the photographs. If you're writing out the text longhand, make sure you leave enough room in your page layout for the journaling. For a little variety, you can write the text at an angle or in other shapes, such as arches or waves.
- You can write your journaling text— captions or paragraphs—on a separate piece of cardstock, cut it out, and then attach it to the page. This allows you to tilt the entire section of text or overlap it with photos on the page, as well as add some contrasting color at the same time. You can also frame the journaling text on an additional piece

tell the stories behind the pictures

of cardstock (in a coordinating color) before mounting it on the page, just as you would a photo.

- Use your journaling to create a border. For example, you can write around the edge of the entire page or around the shape of a photo. Border journaling is a fun way to relate a short incident, include the words of a favorite song, or list miscellaneous adjectives and phrases that you associate with the memories on that page.
- Add journaling inside other page elements, such as die cuts and rubber-stamped images.

IDEAS FOR JOURNALING INFORMATION

Journaling can involve much more than simple names and dates— although that information is certainly important. Here are a few suggestions for things you might include:

- Details describing the who, what, when, where, and why of the photographs.

- The words to favorite songs or poems, including any memories associated with them.
- Descriptions of what you *can't* see in the photos— smells, sounds, textures, and so on.
- Memorabilia such as letters, notes, invitations, or ticket stubs that help tell the story as well as record current prices and styles. (See page 32 for more ideas on collecting memorabilia.)
- Traditions and stories, including favorite recipes, vacation spots, and the like (see page 124).
- A "top ten" list, such as your top ten books, movies, CDs, or restaurants, or a list of highlights from the month, year, or pictured event.
- Local and national events, including leaders, popular movies and fads, sporting events, and current prices. Don't forget about the more personalized facts, such as the floor plan of your home or your car make and model.

You'll find journaling to be one of the most rewarding aspects of creating a scrapbook. Journaling makes your scrapbook much more than a collection of photographs and cute stickers—it gives you a meaningful storybook that will be treasured for generations.

• • • • • Who, What, When, Where, and Why • • • • •

IF YOU'VE EVER SORTED through a pile of unlabeled photographs, you probably know the frustration of trying to remember the details. What year was this picture taken? Who is that person standing next to Grandma? Is this at the park or the campground? Why in the world are these kids dressed up like that? Filling in missing details such as these—especially on older photographs—can be difficult, if not

impossible. That's why it's so important to record this basic information in your scrapbook as well as on the photos themselves. You might think you'll always remember your neighbor's name or when you went to Florida on vacation, but it gets harder the more time passes by.

RECORDING THE FACTS

Each scrapbook page you create should contain details that help identify the photographs. An easy way to remember what kind of information to include is to think of the five W's that reporters use: who, what, when, where, and why.

Who • Identify each person that can be clearly seen in the photographs. Use a nickname if that's how you refer to that person. Try to include the first and last name of anyone who isn't an immediate family member. It's also a good idea to include *every* person's full name at least once somewhere in your scrapbook. It's also helpful to indicate relationships (friend, cousin, next-door neighbor, and so on), as well as the ages of children. If the same person appears in more than one picture on the page, you might decide to label only one of the larger pictures rather than each individual picture.

What • Describe the activity that's taking place in the photographs. Is it a special occasion or holiday? An annual family camp-out or vacation? Add any extra details that help explain what the people in the photos are doing. For example, tell what kind of

cookies are being made, what song is being played at the recital, or what the birthday girl's favorite gift was. The "what" aspect of the photos is often used as part of the page title, since it tells you the subject of the page in a quick glance.

When • Remember to include the date the photos were taken—at least the month and year, if possible. If the photos are from a special event, you might want to include the complete date. For holidays that always fall on the same day, such as Christmas, it's common to only include the year, such as "Christmas 1997." The date can either be a prominent part of the page design (it might even be part of the title) or it can be indicated in a corner of the page. If you have photos on the same page that were taken in different months, try to indicate the date for each photo in a caption.

Where • Another important detail to include is where the photos were taken. This might consist of simply the city and state, or it might be the specific name of a location (such as the name of a restaurant, park, or zoo). The location is especially important to note for pictures taken away from home. Like the date, the location can be a prominent part of your page design or it can be simply written in small print somewhere on the page.

Why • Finally, think about information you can add to your page that will help explain the story behind the pictures. Why is she grinning

Easter Egg Hunt
The Year of the Squirrel

March 30 1997

Laura - age 6

Becky - age 4½

Ben - age 8½

Doug - age 11

Easter morning arrived with the usual forcast of rain. That clever Easter bunny hid the eggs in the forested part of our property, so that if the rain did start while we were at church, the eggs would remain relatively dry. We came home from church, changed clothes and got ready for the hunt. The kids found part of the eggs, but many seemed to be missing. Then we found a chewed up egg shell with the candy gone. Those pesky squirrels had been busy while we were at church and 17 eggs had been stolen! They had good taste too—they left the eggs with peeps and gummy rabbits but took the eggs with the imported English chocolates. We are still finding chewed up eggs two weeks later as they work their way through their stash!

Ben is wearing his traditional Easter expression!

Ready for the hunt!

By Diane Garding, North Bend, Washington. Pens: Sakura Micron Pigma; Pencils: Berol Prisma Color; Stickers: Mrs. Grossman's; Punch: McGill (maple leaf).

like that? Why did you choose that particular vacation spot this year? Why do you enjoy spending time with these friends? This type of journaling is often the most enjoyable to read (and the most fun to write), and is a great way to let the personalities of the subjects in your photos shine.

IDEAS FOR JOURNALING THE DETAILS

Recording the important details in your scrapbook doesn't mean you have to make a "who, what, when, where, why" list on every page. There are lots of fun ways you can include the pertinent facts in your scrapbook. Here are a few ideas for unique, detail-oriented pages:

• Make a family-tree page. You might show the genealogy of a child through photos of parents, grandparents, and great-grandparents. Or, you might have photos of each family from a family reunion.

• Include in your scrapbook a copy of your household calendar—with all its day-to-day reminders. Calendars are a great way to record the activities and events of a busy family. You can reduce the calendar to fit in your album if needed, and there are lots of ways you can dress it up with stickers, die cuts, and other embellishments.

• Create a "The Day I Was Born" page for each family member that lists all the facts, such as the baby's full given name, date and time of birth, hospital and doctor names, and weight and height. Don't forget to include other information such as how long Mom was in labor, what the weather was like, who was the first family member to hear the good news, and so on. You can also add interesting tidbits, such as national events from that day (or month), the total amount of the hospital bill, and contemporary fads or styles.

When you're thinking about adding journaling to a scrapbook page, use the five W's—who, what, when, where, and why—as your guide. Answering these questions will provide valuable facts about the photos, and will get you started thinking about other fun journaling tidbits you might include. Before long, your scrapbook will be your very own personal history book.

• • • Preserving Family Stories and Traditions • • •

EVERY FAMILY HAS a story or two to tell, whether it's an inspiring account of the odd jobs Grandpa took to make ends meet or an amusing tale of a child who went through a "stand on your head" phase. Our family stories connect us to the past and often become more cherished than any material possessions left behind. And there's no better place to record the stories and traditions of your family than in your scrapbook, where they can be remembered and reread frequently and add meaning to your photographs at the same time.

TIPS FOR RECORDING STORIES

Writing down your family's stories and traditions can be one of the most rewarding aspects of scrapbooking. Here are some tips to help you get started:

- In addition to stories from the past, record current happenings in your family. If you don't think you have

any stories to tell, look to your photos for inspiration. As you study the photos on your page, ask yourself questions such as these: Did anything memorable (or funny, sad, embarrassing, etc.) happen just before or after these photos were taken? Is the activity shown associated with a family routine or tradition that could be further explained?

- Remember that you're not being graded on your writing style or sentence structure. Simply write the story down as if you were telling it to a friend. And resist the temptation to embellish your family history. Your stories will be more credible if you tell the facts as they happened—after all, no family is happy all of the time.

- If you're concerned about garbling the story, you can jot down an outline first on a separate piece of paper. You can also write the complete story on a separate piece of paper, and then copy it onto your scrapbook page. This also helps you know how much room you'll need to leave for the story.

- Don't forget to write about the everyday occurrences in your family. Tell about bed-

time routines, working in the yard, what Dad or Mom does at work, and other seemingly ordinary events.

- Interview family members and friends for their memories and stories. You also might find it interesting to get different perspectives on the same event, since people often remember different details.

- Remember to describe the small details that can make the memories and stories more real—feelings, colors, smells, sounds, textures, and so on.

IDEAS FOR ADDING STORIES TO YOUR SCRAPBOOK

Family stories and traditions don't always have to be long paragraphs of text. Here are some ways you can preserve—and enhance—the stories in your scrapbook:

- Create a "family newspaper" page with stories written by different family members. For example, the stories might describe a typical day at your house, include polls of family favorites, list achievements of the past month, or relate the specifics of a special celebration. Take photos to accompany the stories and be sure to include the name and age of each "reporter."

- Include specifics such as your favorite song lyrics or family recipes. These elements can also be used as a fun part of your page decorations. For example, lyrics can be turned into a page or photo border and

interview family and friends

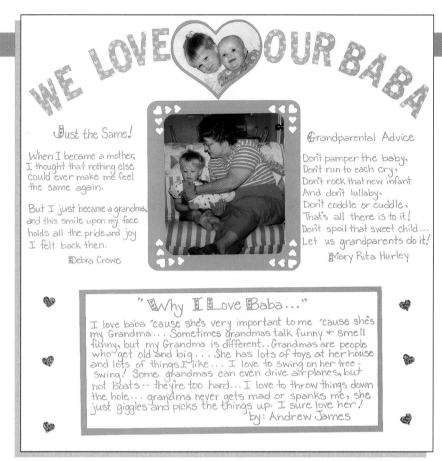

Just the Same!

When I became a mother,
I thought that nothing else
could ever make me feel
the same again.

But I just became a grandma,
and this smile upon my face
holds all the pride and joy
I felt back then.

Debra Crowe

Grandparental Advice

Don't pamper the baby,
Don't run to each cry,
Don't rock that new infant
And don't lullaby,
Don't coddle or cuddle,
That's all there is to it!
Don't spoil that sweet child...
Let us grandparents do it!

Mary Rita Hurley

"Why I Love Baba..."

I love baba 'cause she's very important to me 'cause she's
my Grandma... Sometimes grandmas talk funny + smell
funny, but my Grandma is different.. Grandmas are people
who get old and big... She has lots of toys at her house
and lots of things I like... I love to swing on her tree-
swing! Some grandmas can even drive airplanes, but
not boats -- they're too hard... I love to throw things down
the hole... grandma never gets mad or spanks me, she
just giggles and picks the things up. I sure love her!

by: Andrew James

Pages by and about grandmothers can let everyone enjoy a little bit of the experience! By Ellen James, Pleasant Grove, Utah. Stickers: Design Originals (letters), Mrs. Grossman's (heart); Corner punch: Family Treasures (heart).

recipes can be written on actual recipe cards. Be sure to describe any associated memories, such as when you remember singing a specific song or your first experience cooking a family recipe.

- Add details to your wedding pages— your feelings and fears on the big day, problems that came up, what was served at the reception, your first apartment or house, and so on. Tell the story of how you met your spouse and how you got engaged. What qualities attracted you to your spouse? Did you have a favorite song? What was your best date?

- Include a local map that correlates with the date of the photos on the page. Describe your neighborhood and any favorite hang-outs, and take photos of current landmarks and buildings. You can also create pages that highlight the homes

you've lived in throughout the years. List the reasons why you chose each home, the purchase price, and how long you lived there.

- Use a combination of photos and journaling to chronicle your family traditions. For example, you might record how you spend Christmas or Easter morning, how you celebrate birthdays, or where you like to go on vacation—or how you decide where to go each year.

- Take photographs of family heirlooms and then describe their original owners and how they came into your possession. Include favorite stories about ancestors on the page.

Whether your family stories are simple, funny, heartwarming, or even a little strange, they will make your scrapbook the most intriguing and interesting biography your children and grandchildren will ever read!

Interview Questions

INTERVIEWS ARE A GREAT WAY to gather your family's stories so you can transfer them to your scrapbook. Older family members will likely have more stories to tell, but the responses from children can often be quite insightful. Here are a few examples of questions you might ask:

- What were your favorite childhood games and toys?

- Tell me about a time you got in trouble. What was your punishment?

- Have you ever had a nickname, and if so, how did you get it?

- What activities or sports do you enjoy participating in and why?

- What do you remember about your grandparents or great-grandparents?

- What was the first job you ever had? How did you get it? What did you like or dislike about it?

- What were the clothing fads when you were in junior high or high school?

- What is the scariest (or most amazing, most embarrassing, etc.) thing that has ever happened to you?

- What is the funniest practical joke you've ever played on someone (or someone has played on you)?

- What is your favorite story about a pet you've had?

- How did you choose your current line of work? Or, what kind of work would you most enjoy doing?

- Who is the most mischievous member of your family? The biggest tease? The most frugal? The hardest worker? The most creative?

• • Recording the Words of a Child • • • • •

PARTY! CAKE!

CHILDREN ENJOY a unique perspective on the world around them, which frequently causes adults to laugh, sigh, or simply stand back in amazement. Without writing these funny and profound quips down, you'll have a hard time remembering them years down the road. Recording the words and thoughts of children in your scrapbook

is a wonderful way to capture a little bit of their personalities and at the same time hold on to some of their innocence and wonder.

ADDING CHILDREN'S WORDS TO YOUR SCRAPBOOK

There are several different techniques you can use to include a child's words in your scrapbook—no matter how old the child is. Here are a few ideas:

Toddlers • For a child who is just learning how to talk, you might simply keep track of the first words spoken and then create a page with that list, along with a photo of the child and his or her age. When children begin to speak in phrases, you can ask them simple questions about an event and then record both the questions and their answers on a page.

Preschoolers • Preschool-aged children (3–5 years old) often become little

chatterboxes who will gladly express their thoughts to anyone willing to listen. You can ask children of this age to explain what's happening in the photographs on the page, and then write down their responses exactly as they give them—grammatical errors and all. Birthdays are a great time to interview kids about their favorite things (colors, TV shows, foods, hobbies, etc.), their friends, their school activities, and their goals for the future. Have them write their name on the page if they can, or draw their own illustrations.

Grade-Schoolers • When children are old enough to write, hand them a pen and let them record their memories in their own handwriting. Or, you might let them type their thoughts on the computer. Don't worry about spelling or punctuation mistakes—these give you an accurate picture of

Interviewing Children

AN EASY WAY TO GET the thoughts of a child is to interview him or her. Here are a few examples of questions you might ask:

• What are your favorite and least favorite subjects in school?

• What is your favorite food? What is your favorite breakfast, lunch, and dinner?

• Who are your best friends? Why do you like to spend time with them?

• What is your favorite thing to do in your free time?

• If you could wear what you wanted to school every day, what would you wear?

• Do you like to play any sports? What do you like about those sports?

• What have you done that you're the proudest of?

• Where is your favorite place to go on vacation? Why?

• What do you want to do when you grow up? Why?

• What did you like best about our trip to the museum (or zoo, park, etc.)?

• What are you looking forward to doing next year?

• What are you going to do right after we finish talking?

their development at that point and will provide lots of smiles when they look back on the page in the future. You can also interview kids at this age or have them dictate an explanation of the photos to you.

Preteens and Teenagers • By the time they're teenagers, many kids have already started their own scrapbooks, which is a wonderful way for them to record their thoughts, feelings, and aspirations. Of course, you can still ask your teenagers about their memories and favorite things to add to your pages.

IDEAS FOR CHILDREN'S PAGES

In addition to interviews and lists of favorite things, there are lots of fun ways to capture a child's unique personality in a scrapbook. Here are a few ideas:

• Include the funny and cute things your children say. You might even devote an entire page to their memorable quotes and mispronunciations. Write down their words on a notepad or your calendar as soon as possible so you don't forget them, and then transfer them later to your scrapbook page. These quotes make great photo captions; they can also be used to fill up extra space on the page. Try to include photos of activities that are related to specific expressions the children use frequently.

• Have a child draw a self-portrait or a family portrait for your scrapbook. Doing this on each birthday is a great way to see how their perceptions of themselves (as well as their artistic abilities) change from year to year.

• Ask a younger child to write down (or dictate to you) the steps for an everyday task, such as raking the lawn, baking cookies, or making a bed. Include a picture of the child participating in that activity.

• Use the child's artwork and schoolwork to decorate your scrapbook pages. You can cut up portions of the drawing or assignment to add to your page, or you can include the entire piece in a pocket page (see page 78). If you're worried about the quality of the original paper, make a color copy first on acid-free paper.

• Hand over some duplicate photographs and a few supplies, and put the kids to work creating their own scrapbook pages. You can keep the completed pages in your album or start the children's very own scrapbooks. Encourage the children to add journaling to the pages they create to describe their thoughts and feelings. Older kids might even have their own cameras, such as disposable ones, to take pictures for their scrapbooks.

Preserving the words of children at all ages creates a wonderful record of their growth and development. When the children are grown, they'll receive great enjoyment from looking back through the pages of your scrapbook, reading some of their youthful words and thoughts, and reliving a little part of their childhood.

By Kristie Silvester, Roy, Utah. Paper: Close to my Heart (red plaid and recipe cards), Carson-Dellosa (sandwich); Scissors: Fiskars (Wave); Die Cuts: Ellison (large ant); Corner rounder: Carl Punches; Rubber Stamps on cards: D.O.T.S. and Marvy Brush markers; Small ants: Kristie's own design.

By Jackie Morley, Las Vegas, Nevada. Paper: The Paper Patch, Mary Englebreit; Pens: Zig Writer; Scissors: Fiskars (Zipper); Stickers: Mary Englebreit.

• • • • • • • • Journaling for Hard Times • • • • • • • •

SCRAPBOOKS PROVIDE a wonderful way to preserve life's joyful, happy moments. But sometimes life has a way of throwing a wrench into things and disrupting our peace and calm. During these difficult periods, our scrapbooks can be a great source of comfort. Through our scrapbooks— and especially through journaling— we can find strength and solace as we deal with whatever obstacles are placed in our path.

USING SCRAPBOOKS TO HELP THE HEALING PROCESS

Scrapbooks can play an important part in helping to heal our hearts and our families after a tragic loss, whether

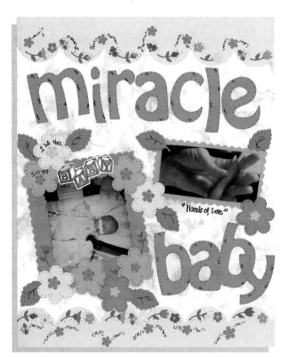

By Brenda Hall, Yuma, Arizona. Brenda's scrapbook pages about her premature daughter remind Brandi, now a healthy schoolgirl, of her own brave spirit.

it's the loss of life, health, or our home.

Death • Through scrapbooks, we can pay tribute to a loved one who has passed on after living a rich, full life. Scrapbooks can help us remember the many lives touched by a sister or daughter who was taken before her time. We can express our grief at the loss of a child along with the sweetness and joy that child brought into the home. Creating a memorial album for a loved one who has died can help us work through our grief, while at the same time helping us preserve and share the memory of that special person for future family members.

Illness or Injury • When someone close to us is fighting a serious illness or recovering from a tragic accident, our scrapbooks give us a way to record the daily struggles—the ups as well as the downs—and carry us through the hardest moments. Chronicling the highs and lows of a seriously ill or injured family member can give us strength and courage. On those days that seem particularly tough, reading back through the entries in our scrapbook pages is sometimes all we need to lift our spirits. And if the blessing of a recovery occurs, we'll have an inspiring account of deter-

mination and courage to share with others.

Natural Disasters • After a devastating disaster such as a flood, fire, or tornado, our scrapbooks can mark a starting-over point in our lives. We can record not only the historical data of the disaster itself but also the steps we take to rebuild our homes and our lives.

IDEAS FOR RECORDING DIFFICULT TIMES IN YOUR SCRAPBOOK

While each of us must find the method for dealing with tragic events and difficult circumstances that works best, there are several ways that scrapbooks can be helpful. Here are a few ideas for recording hard times in your scrapbook:

- Use journaling to record your thoughts, feelings, and experiences—both good and bad. Journaling can be very therapeutic and is often one of the best ways to work through grief and pain. If you've lost a loved one, you can recall some of your favorite memories of that person or write down your hopes and dreams for what might have been. You can also record things such as the kind deeds performed by others for you or your family.

- If you're trying to cope with the death of a loved one, you might write him or her a letter. Letters can help you sort through the many emotions you're feeling and help you say good-bye. If you feel it's

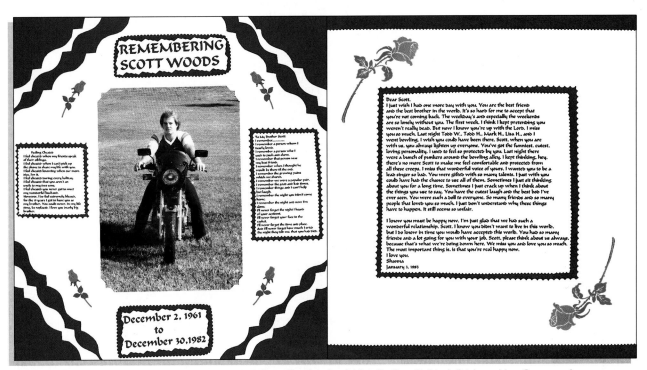

By Shana Dill, Grover Beach, California. Scissors: Fiskars (Scallop, Leaf, Mini-Scallop, Pinking); Stickers: Mrs. Grossman's.

appropriate, you might choose to display the letter in your scrapbook.

- You can create a beautiful memorial album by asking family members and friends to send scrapbook pages paying tribute to the person who has died. They might share their favorite memories of the person or describe the qualities they admired most. Placing all of these pages in one album is a wonderful way to remember how much that person was loved.

- If you want to record some of your feelings and emotions but don't necessarily want others to read them, consider putting together two separate albums. One album might contain tributes and photos that are appropriate for everyone to read and share, while the other album might be more like a private journal.

- Look for poetry or song lyrics that you can add to your scrapbook pages. There are many beautiful pieces that deal with different tragedies and can often express the feelings in your heart.

- Include appropriate memorabilia, such as notes and cards of sympathy, hospital bracelets, or pressed flowers. If you're not up to putting together your scrapbook pages right away, save the special items together in a box until you're ready. You might also want to save any journaling notes you've written to help you remember what you were feeling at the time.

- Find someone who has been through a similar experience. Not only can you be a great support for each other, but you can share ideas as well.

While we naturally focus on the happy times of life, no family is without occasional sadness. It is the combination of all the joys and sorrows we experience that defines who we are and creates the legacy that we pass down to our posterity. Scrapbooks offer us a unique opportunity to preserve—and present—this legacy and family history as we could in no other way.

Valentines day was so fun. We had a candle light dinner, Then we went on a carriage ride, and while we were on it, Ben asked me to marry him and gave me my ring. It is so pretty.

Then we went and saw Titanic again. I love that movie. After we went and showed everyone my ring. We had such a fun night.

1998

Valentines day.

AN
Idea Book FOR
Inspiration

Try great new page ideas in your own scrapbook

I am continually amazed at the freshness of the scrapbooking ideas I see—a new way to use a punch, great ideas for composing photos, color combinations I've never thought of. While occasionally I think up a brilliant idea for my scrapbook, usually the brilliant ideas in my scrapbooks come from other scrapbookers!

In this section are 60 brand-new scrapbook pages and spreads from the best-of-the-best scrapbookers. Look how they frame their photos and match paper patterns. See how they incorporate memorabilia and items from nature. Notice when they leave room to write a long story, and when just a headline is enough. And pay close attention to the themes they've chosen—sometimes stories from everyday life make the best pages! Most important, have fun using them as inspiration for your own scrapbook pages. Happy scrapbooking!

By Karen Stott, Salt Lake City, Utah. Paper: The Paper Patch; Sticker paper: Sandylion (sparkly diamond); Font: Scrap Heart, "Lettering Delights," Inspire Graphics. (See Index for complete spread.)

By Terina Darcey. Paper: source unknown; Scissors: Family Treasures; Paper Crimper: Fiskars.

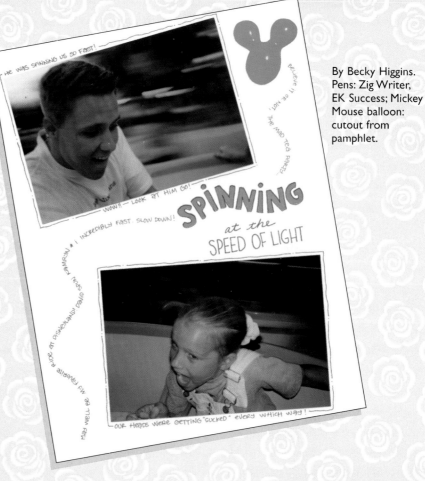

By Becky Higgins. Pens: Zig Writer, EK Success; Mickey Mouse balloon: cutout from pamphlet.

By Deanna Lambson. Paper: Little Extras (polka dot); Scissors: Fiskars (Pinking); "Let's Go Play" cut out: from Disneyland brochure.

By Becky Higgins. Pens: Zig Writer, EK Success; Stickers: Sandylion (Disney, boat, pirate, Goofy), Mrs. Grossman's (train, star, money, binoculars, and skeleton), Mary Engelbreit, Melissa Neufeld, Inc.(teapot).

By Stacy Julian.
Paper: source
unknown; Photo
Corners: Canson-
Talens.

By Karen Stott.
Paper: MM's Design.

By Karen Stott.
Paper: Mara-mi;
Die Cuts: Ellison.

Megan is our bundle of joy!

MEGAN

By Stacy Julian.
Paper: Penny Laine;
Scissors: Fiskars
(Stamp).

Read All About It ...

My Dad

My Mom

May 9, 1965

STACY PATRICIA HALL is the new daughter of Mr. and Mrs. Farley Briggs Hall of South Fairway. She was born May 6. Mr. Hall is a WSU student in vet medicine.

May 15, 1966

November 12, 1994

and me ↑

MITCHELL, INDIANA, MAY 19.

Births and Illnesses

Mr. and Mrs. Gary Julian, California, are parents of a son, Geoffrey Garrison, grandparents are Mr. and Mrs. Russell Julian of Mitchell.

UTAH BIRTHS

By Beth Whitmarsh.
Paper: The Paper
Patch. Watermelon
seeds were made
with a McGill heart
punch and then
cut in half.

By Karen Stott.
Paper: The Paper
Patch; Die Cuts:
Scrap Ease, What's
New, Ltd.

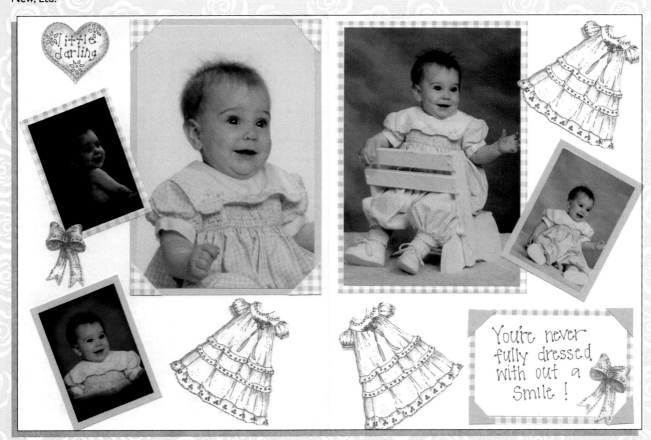

M E G A N

Nothing's as precious, or brings so much love, as a brand new baby sent from above!

Age 5 weeks

By Jenny Curtis.
Paper: Provo Craft;
Fonts: D.J. Blocks, D.J. Inkers.

A baby's love is the best of all!
Mommy and Megan

By Karen Stott.
Paper: Penny Laine.

By Lisa Bearnson. Stickers: Frances Meyer; Lettering Template: PebblesTracers, Pebbles in My Pocket; Corner Die Cuts: What's New, Ltd.

By Barbara Tanner. Paper: Mara-mi; Scissors: Fiskars (Jigsaw); Die Cuts: Accu-Cut Systems.

By Becky Higgins.
Paper: Paper Pizazz,
Hot Off The Press;
Sticker: Mrs.
Grossman's.

By Tracy White.
Scissors: Fiskars
(Deckle); Die Cut:
Creative Memories;
Paper Crimper:
Fiskars; Template:
Provo Craft.

By Karen Stott.
Stickers: Mrs.
Grossman's.

HANGING
OUT
WITH THE
GIRLS —
HANNAH,
RUTHANN,
AND
AMELIA

PLAYING
DRESS-UP

GIRLS WILL BE
GIRLS

By Becky Higgins.
Paper: The Paper
Patch; Stickers:
Mrs. Grossman's.

Kendra and Jake
have a lot of fun
playing in their
tree house. Jake
and dad built it
together.

October 1997

By Jenny Curtis.
Die Cuts: Accu-Cut
Systems; Fonts:
Scrap Wood,
Inspire Graphics.

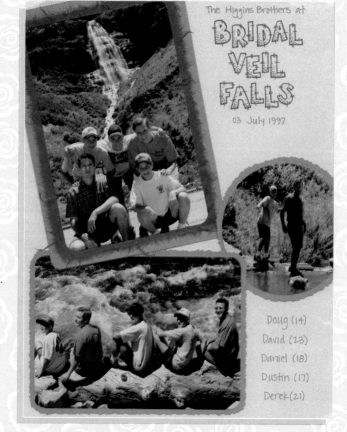

The Higgins Brothers at
BRIDAL
VEIL
FALLS
03 July 1997

Doug (14)
David (23)
Daniel (18)
Dustin (17)
Derek (21)

By Becky Higgins.
Paper: Personal
Stamp Exchange
(mulberry); Pens:
Zig Writer, EK
Success; Scissors:
Family Treasures
(Deckle).

By Lisa Bearnson. Stickers: Frances Meyer; Lettering Template: Pebbles Tracers, Pebbles in My Pocket.

WATER BUG Kade

During the summer of 1996 Kade surprised us one day by washing the van all by himself. He even laid on the asphalt and washed underneath. He was soaked from head to toe. What a Kid!!
Another day it was raining cats and dogs. Once again we found Kade outside. He was roller blading in the rain with a huge umbrella over his head.

By Stacy Julian. Paper: Close to My Heart.

SNIPS and

SNails and PUPPY dog TAILS...

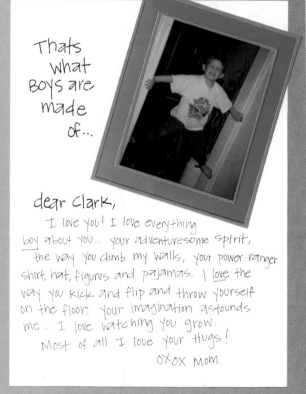

Thats what BOYS are made of...

dear Clark,
I love you! I love everything boy about you... your adventuresome spirit, the way you climb my walls, your power-ranger shirt, hat, figures and pajamas. I love the way you kick and flip and throw yourself on the floor. Your imagination astounds me... I love watching you grow.
Most of all I love your Hugs!
OXOX Mom.

By Barbara Tanner.
Paper: Memory Press;
Paper Crimper:
Fiskars; Other:
Christmas card.

Reed and Sara 1982 ♡

Posing with the tree we
decorated for Great
Grandma Tanner!

By Becky Higgins.
Paper: Main Street
Press, Ltd.; Pens:
Zig Writer,
EK Success;
Scissors: Family
Treasures (Deckle).

By Becky Higgins.
Paper: Personal
Stamp Exchange
(mulberry); Pens:
Zig Writer,
EK Success;
Stencil: Provo
Craft (star).

By Becky Higgins. Paper:
The Paper Patch;
Scissors: Fiskars (Mini-Scallop).
Die Cut: Ellison

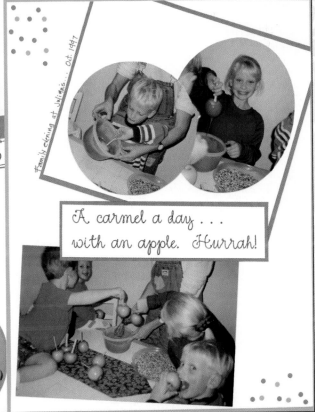

By Terina Darcey. Die Cut: Accu-Cut
Systems; Punch: Fiskars; Fonts: D.J.
Blocks and D.J. Fancy, D.J. Inkers.

By Becky Higgins.
Paper: Main Street
Press, Ltd.; Other:
dried foliage.

By Becky Higgins.
Paper: source
unknown.

By Becky Higgins.
Paper: from Mary
Engelbreit day
calendar; Pencils:
Prisma Color;
Die Cuts: Ellison.

David, Ian, Terina, Dia and Grampa Bill
Spent the day chasing lizards,
sloshing in mud and wading in water
up to our knees.

Just generally having a great time!

LEAPIN' LIZARDS !

Southern Utah 1997
Little Wild Horse

By Terina Darcey.
Paper: Provo Craft
(green speckle);
Lizards: MM's Design;
Fonts: D.J. Desert,
D.J. Inkers.

THE "Y" MOUNTAIN

a look at
WASATCH
FRONT
in autumn

THESE PHOTOGRAPHS WERE
TAKEN ON 21 OCTOBER 1997
FROM BYU CAMPUS IN
PROVO, UTAH. BEAUTIFUL!!

MOUNT
TIMPANOGOS

By Becky Higgins.
Pen: Zig Writer,
EK Success; Pencils:
Prisma Color; Other:
leaves are preserved
in contact paper.

By Tracy White. Punches:
Family Treasures.

By Tracy White. Template:
Provo Craft.

By Tracy White. Stickers:
Frances Meyer (butterfly),
Melissa Neufeld, Inc. (cat);
Rubber Stamp: Personal
Stamp Exchange.

By Terina Darcey. Paper:
Provo Craft; Fonts: D.J. Crayon,
D.J. Inkers.

By Tracy White. Paper: Personal Stamp Exchange (mulberry); Photo Corners: Pebbles in My Pocket.

THE FAMILY MY GRANDMOTHER GREW UP IN...

HER FATHER: CHARLIE (CHAS)

HER MOTHER: EMMA SUSAN

ELDEST BROTHER: ELBERT ELWOOD

OTHER BROTHER: CHARLES DAVID

ESTHER JANE CARLSON WAS BORN 19 OCT. 1915

By Becky Higgins. Paper: Personal Stamp Exchange (maroon mulberry); Paper with grass blades was handmade by Becky; Other: dried foliage.

6 months

By Beth Whitmarsh. Paper: The Paper Patch.

allie

July 4th @ Grandmas 1997

"mommy's little star!!"

By Allison Myers. Paper: Northern Spy Faux Designs Imprintables; Stickers: Mrs. Grossman's; Letter Stickers: Making Memories.

By Jenny Jackson.
Scissors: Fiskars
(Peak).

March - May 1997
"The Winner School"

Doggone Good
Award
Presented to
Zach

Zach's first experience
in Preschool was at
the Winner School in
Salt Lake City. His
teacher was Miss Julie
and he had a little
crush on her!!!

ZACH

One of his favorite
subjects in school was art.
He always came home with
beautiful artwork to decorate the

By Terina Darcey.
Paper: Provo Craft;
Die Cuts: Accu-Cut
Systems (apples);
Ellison (frame).

ABC
2+2=4

abcdefghijklmnopqrstuvwxyz

Back 2 School

abcdefghijklmnopqrstuvwxyzß

abcdefghijklmnopqrstuvwxyzß

Diondra
Elizabeth
Darcey

Carden
Memorial
School
1997

Dia
Lower
Preparatory

$aving for college!

ADORABLE INITIATIVE!

Lemonade 10¢

SEEMINGLY INNOCENT, WONDERFULLY INVENTIVE, AND STRICTLY HONEST GROUP OF YOUNG ENTREPRENEURS.

NOT!

By Terina Darcey. Die Cuts: Ellison; Font: D.J. Crayon and D.J. Bassoon, D.J. Inkers; Rubber Stamp: D.O.T.S. (lips); Tissue-paper money: Masterpiece.

DUSTIN and DANIEL are ready for PROM NIGHT!!

DUSTIN - AGE 17

DANIEL - AGE 18

Daniel Kimball Higgins Class of '97

By Becky Higgins. Paper: Personal Stamp Exchange (mulberry); Pens: Zig Writer, EK Success, Micron Pigma, Sakura.

PLAY BALL!

Derek & Clancy
August 1997
Connie Mack
World Series

By Karen Stott.
Paper: Provo Craft;
Baseballs: The
Paper Patch.

07 JUNE 1997

tennis

DAVID & BECKY, STEVEN & ELINN, KEVIN, AND DAVID

By Becky Higgins.
Pens: Zig Writer,
EK Success; Stickers:
Paper House
Productions
(tennis ball).

By Lisa Bearnson.
Punches: Family Trea-
sures (large circle),
McGill (small circle).

Anyone up for a game
of golf? At our July
4th '97 Dorris family
reunion the Broderick's
planned a game of
golf with real golf clubs
and plastic golf balls.
One of the relays was to
see who could hit their
ball the farthest. The
winners? Steve in the
adult category and
Mallon (age 14) in
the child's game.

By Karen Stott.
Paper: The Paper
Patch; Stationery:
Provo Craft;
Template:
Provo Craft.

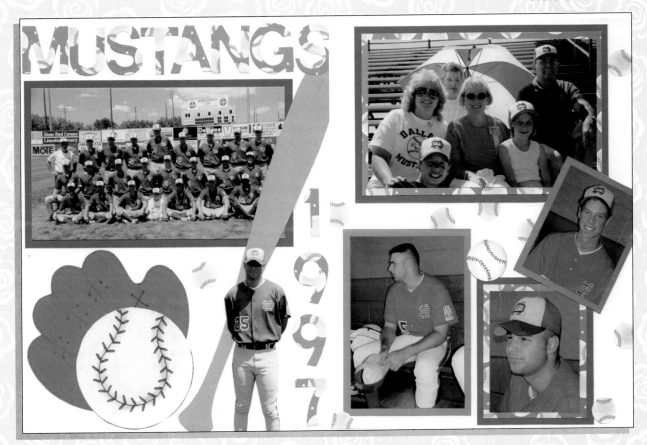

We sat behind

STEVE YOUNG

at the basketball game.

as i held the camera, waiting to get a good shot of him, he looked right at the camera for no reason (very candid & very random!) i snapped & the timing was great— what luck!

ON JANUARY 17, 1998 we went to a BYU basketball game at the Marriott Center.

BYU lost, but we had a great time with the Nordfelt's & Kennedy's!

after the game... Frontier Pies!

a little out of focus, but the only photo i have of the 6 of us!

COUGAR BASKETBALL
BRIGHAM YOUNG UNIVERSITY
MARRIOTT CENTER
BYU VS COLORADO STATE
7:00 P.M.
SAT. JANUARY 17, 1998

By Becky Higgins. Paper: Paper Pizazz, Hot Off The Press (basketball); Pen: Zig Opaque Writer, EK Success; Pencils: Prisma Color; Sticker: Paper House Productions (basketball).

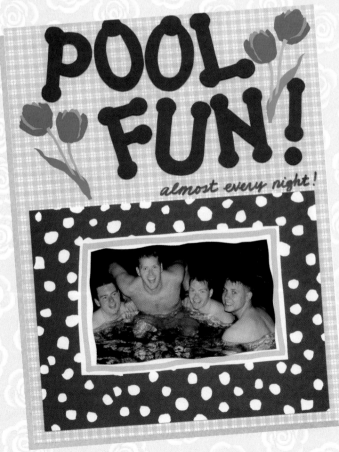

POOL FUN!

almost every night!

By Becky Higgins. Paper: The Paper Patch; Stickers: Mrs. Grossman's; Lettering: Pebbles Tracers, Pebbles in My Pocket (Pool Fun).

By Karen Stott.
Paper: Paper Pizazz,
Hot Off The Press;
Stickers: Frances
Meyer.

By Deanna Lambson.
Pens: Zig Clean
Color, EK
Success; Scissors:
Fiskars (Deckle;
Majestic for photo
corners); Lettering:
Pebbles Tracers,
Pebbles in My Pocket.

By Deanna Lambson.
Pens: Micron Pigma,
Sakura; Scissors:
Fiskars (Scallop);
Lettering: *ABC's of
Creative Lettering*,
Lindsay Ostrom;
Starfish: Deanna's
own design.

By Becky Higgins.
Paper: Paper Pizazz,
Hot Off The Press;
Pencils: Prisma Color.

Vacations should be good enough to be fun, but bad enough that you look forward to home!
...Terina Darcey, 1997

Camping is an ideal vacation!
Little Wild Horse Crack Canyon, 1997

By Terina Darcey.
Paper: Close to
My Heart; Fonts:
D.J. Desert, D.J.
Inkers.

By Karen Stott.
Paper: Wubie Prints;
Templates:
Provo Craft.

LAKE

POWELL

Jake and Josh
having fun,
at Lake Powell
August 1997

By Becky Higgins.
Paper: Personal Stamp
Exchange (mulberry);
Pens: Zig Writer,
EK Success; Stickers:
Mrs. Grossman's;
Photo Corner
Stickers: Frances
Meyer.

By Becky Higgins.
Pen: Zig Clean Color,
EK Success; Other:
map of zoo.

RESOURCE GUIDE

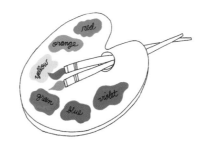

Retreats, Workshops, and Conventions

The ABC Directory of Art & Craft Events
PO Box 5388, Maryville, TN 37802
800/678-3566   FAX: 423/681-4733
A directory of U.S. art and craft events

Auntie Amy Stamps!
6500 Streeter Ave., Riverside, CA 92504
909/689-2530
Scrapbook and rubber stamp conventions
held in regional locations.

Camp Crop: Weekend Retreats
27637 Woodfield Place, Valencia CA 91354
805/296-7732   FAX: 805/296-1950
Relaxing weekend retreats emphasizing
pampering, personal attention, creative
expression, and new scrapbooking ideas.

The Great American Scrapbook Company
PO Box 29250, Lewisville, TX 75067
972/318-0492   FAX: 972/318-0491
scrapbkc@gte.net
The world's largest yearly scrapbook convention.

Memories Expo
PO Box 3388, Zanesville, OH 43702-3388
740/452-4541   FAX: 740/452-2552
Runs scrapbook conventions across the country.

Midwest Scrapbook Convention
221 Jefferson St. N., Wadena, MN 56482
218/631-4966   FAX: 218/631-4966
Runs scrapbook conventions across the country.

Scrapbooker's Dream Day
PO Box 183, Hyde Park, UT 84318
FAX: 801/393-8856
The annual Utah scrapbook convention.

The Scrapbook Expo
PO Box 98, Corona, CA 91718
888/252-EXPO
Scrapbook conventions with locations across
the country.

Scrapbook Getaways
PO Box 3787, Logan, UT 84323-3787
888/755-5933   FAX: 888/755-5933
Weekend retreats at resorts featuring classes and
contests.

SI Productions
2631 N. Woodrow Ave., Simi Valley, CA 93065
805/520-0304
Scrapbooking workshops and education held in
regional locations.

Rankin Ranch
PO Box 36, Caliente, CA 93518
805/867-2511   FAX: 805/864-0105
Retreats held in a family owned guest ranch deep
in the Tehachapi mountains in California.

Home Demonstrations and Workshops

Close To My Heart
738 East Quality Drive,
American Fork, UT 84003

888/655-6552   FAX: 801/763-8188
Scrapbook supply company with in-home
demonstrators.

D.O.T.S.
738 East Quality Drive, American Fork,
UT 84003
888/655-6552 FAX: 801/763-8188
Rubber stamp company with in-home
demonstrators.

Stampin' Up
800/STAMPUP   www.stampinup.com
Rubber stamp company with in-home
demonstrators.

Mail Order/Catalogs

Albums by Design
PO Box 265, Valleyford, WA 99036
509/891-4124
A full line of acid-free scrapbooking supplies; you
can earn free supplies by holding catalog parties.

Artistic Albums & More
26741 Portola Parkway, Suite 1E-416,
Foothill Ranch, CA 92610
888/9-ALBUMS   FAX: 714/888-5782
A catalog selling acid-free scrapbook supplies
at discounts.

The Cropping Corner, Inc.
800/608-2467   FAX: 303/692-0639
http://www.croppingcorner.com
Photosafe scrapbooking supplies sold online.

Gentle Creations
1140 NW Lester Ave., Corvallis OR 97330
800/682-3712   www.stickervilleusa.com
Complete line of Mrs. Grossman's acid-free
stickers.

Heartstrings Network Scrapbook Supplies
909/593-9902   FAX: 909/596-0603
http://home.earthlink.net/~heartstrings
All the latest scrapbooking supplies sold online.

Keeping Memories Alive
800/419-4949   FAX: 800/947-3609
www.scrapbooks.com
Complete line of scrapbook supplies.

Kozy Memories
6006 Marsh Hawk Ct., Elk Grove, CA 95758
916/683-5090   FAX: 916/684-8730
Quality scrapbook supplies for less.

Lest We Forget
9 El Morro, Rancho Santa Margarita, CA 92688
888/811-6533   FAX: 714/459-6307
A catalog selling a complete line of scrapbook
supplies at discounts.

Memories By Design
1771 N. Main St. Suite #4, Layton, UT 84041
888/SCRAP88   FAX: 801/775-9320
A catalog selling the newest scrapbooking
products.

Memory Maniacs
16184 Wedgeworth Dr.,
Hacienda Heights, CA 91745-2937
888/521-2582
A club providing scrapbooking supplies at
discounts.

Pebbles in my Pocket
800/438-8153
http://www.pebblesinmypocket.com
Affordable scrapbooking and stationery supplies.

Remember Me Scrapbooking
#103-250 Schoolhouse St.,
Coquitlam, BC V3K 6V7
800/451-7086 FAX: 604/520-1193
www.remembermesb.com
Online and mail-order source, with offices
in the U.S. and Canada.

Rocky Mountain Craft
540 E. 500 N., American Fork, UT 84003
800/270-9130   FAX: 801/756-0577
A complete line of scrap supplies.

The Scrap Patch
PO Box 645, Mendon, MI 49072
FAX: 616/496-8315
www.iboutique.com/scrappatch/
Color cardstock in 12" x 12" size. Send SASE for
catalog.

Scrapbook Supplies on the Internet
www.scrapbooksupplies.com
Extensive catalog with discount prices and
helpful hints.

Scrapbooker's Paradise Mail Order
2001 -10th Ave. SW, Calgary, Alberta T3C 0K4
888/636-8818   FAX: 403/245-2704
A full line of scrapbooking supplies.

Stampin' and Scrappin'
5610 District Blvd #107, Bakersfield, CA 93313
800/810-0772   www.stampinscrappin.com
Online catalog with low prices.

Sticker Planet
10736 Jefferson Boulevard, Sticker Station 503,
Culver City, CA 90230
800/557-8678   www.stickerplanet.com
A color catalog featuring more than 350 sticker
designs.

Victorian House
577 S. Main St., Bourbonnais, IL 60911
888/400-6043
Webway albums and full assortment of
scrapbooking supplies.

INDEX

By Barbara Silvester. See page 11 for supply list.

by Angelyn Bryce. See page 35 for supply list.

1998

Valentines day was so fun. We had a candle light dinner. Then we went on a carriage ride, and while we were on it, Ben asked me to marry him and gave me my ring. It is so pretty.

Then we went and saw Titanic again. I love that movie. After we went and showed everyone my ring. We had such a fun night.

Valentines day.

By Karen Stott. See page 131 for supply list.

• • • • • • • • • • **Acknowledgments** • • • • • • • • • • •
Memories are a result of the diverse experiences we encounter every day, and writing a book is definitely a memorable event. Fortunately, the rewarding memories of this project far outweigh the struggles, thanks in great part to the many people who willingly gave of their time and talents every step along the way. We are grateful to the outstanding team that helped make this book a reality. Our thanks especially go to Maureen Graney, president of Blackberry Press, for her vision and encouragement from beginning to end. Others at Blackberry Press are also well deserving of our praise, especially Carmile Zaino, Jackie Pardo, Kevin Callahan, and the editorial team. We also express thanks to the folks at Oxmoor House for their creativity and energy, especially Johnny McIntosh, pub-lisher, and Nancy Wyatt, editor-in-chief, for enthusiastically signing up our book, and to Dianne Mooney, vice-president of development, Gary Wright, head of publicity; and Jennifer Brunnemer in promotion for bringing it to life. Several hard-working individuals at *Creating Keepsakes* magazine contributed much to this project, including Don Lambson, who freely shared his design expertise, Amy Tippetts and Celeste Rockwood-Jones, who helped acquire and scan sample page layouts, and Kim San-doval, whose coordination skills kept everything running smoothly. We couldn't have completed this book without the support and encourage-ment of our families. Our heartfelt love and thanks to Brian (who belongs to Gayle) and Steve (who belongs to Lisa). And finally, we wish to thank children everywhere—especially those near and dear to our hearts—who constantly remind us why it's so important to make and record memories.
—Lisa Bearnson and Gayle Humpherys